Abraham Kuyper, Conservatism, and Church and State

Abraham Kuyper, Conservatism, and Church and State

Mark J. Larson

WIPF & STOCK · Eugene, Oregon

ABRAHAM KUYPER, CONSERVATISM, AND CHURCH AND STATE

Copyright © 2015 Mark J. Larson. All rights reserved. Except for brief quotations in critical publications or reviews, no part of this book may be reproduced in any manner without prior written permission from the publisher. Write: Permissions. Wipf and Stock Publishers, 199 W. 8th Ave., Suite 3, Eugene, OR 97401.

Wipf & Stock
An Imprint of Wipf and Stock Publishers
199 W. 8th Ave., Suite 3
Eugene, OR 97401

www.wipfandstock.com

ISBN 13: 978-1-4982-1956-3

Manufactured in the U.S.A.   09/28/2015

For Dad, Mom, and Edward

Contents

Preface | ix
Introduction | xi

1 Conservatism | 1
2 God and Humanity | 13
3 Limited Government | 23
4 Church and State | 34
5 Madisonian | 48
6 Tyranny | 60
7 Resistance and Reform | 74
Conclusion | 95

Bibliography | 99
Subject Index | 109

Preface

IN MY OFFICE HANGS a large framed photograph of the Dutch theologian Abraham Kuyper, an encouragement to biblical fidelity and growth in grace and knowledge. My journey in the study of Kuyper's theology began with the reading of his devotional writings. His biblical expositions touched my heart, drawing my soul into a deeper communion with Christ through the power of the gospel. I then moved to an examination of his work in biblical commentary and systematic theology. His commentary on Revelation led me to a renewed commitment to a literal hermeneutic in the interpretation of biblical prophecy. His volume on the Holy Spirit, in my judgment, is still one of the monumental works on the subject of pneumatology. I turned my attention at last to his treatment of political theory. His lecture on Calvinism and politics delivered at Princeton Theological Seminary in 1898 has had a profound impact upon me, shaping and giving direction to my thinking on political theory.

It has been my privilege in recent years to attend the annual Kuyper Conference on the beautiful campus of Princeton Theological Seminary to fellowship with the finest students of Kuyper in our time. I am grateful for every scholar, for their penetrating intellects and for their enthusiasm in exploring Kuyper's theology and its implications for our generation. There can surely be no better location for such a meeting of Kuyper enthusiasts, the same venue in which Kuyper gave his famous lectures on Calvinism in the Miller Chapel, still a sanctuary for meditation, prayer, and worship.

Preface

Let me express my appreciation for four scholars in particular. James McGoldrick, my former history professor at Cedarville University, first alerted me to the importance of Kuyper when he informed me in the early 1990s that he was writing a biography on him. Later, when taking a doctoral seminar with James Bratt at Calvin Theological Seminary, the importance of Kuyper was further underscored when he likewise mentioned that he was engaged in Kuyper research and writing. At the same time, John Bolt published a volume on Kuyper that further piqued my interest. Following my doctoral studies, I attended the annual conference at Princeton hosted by the Abraham Kuyper Center for Public Theology. While there, I had the pleasure of meeting John Halsey Wood, a young Kuyper scholar, at the time a doctoral student in historical theology at Saint Louis University. His work further encouraged me to proceed in my own research. I have benefited immensely from these four gentlemen, all of whom have made significant contributions in the field of Kuyper studies.

I am especially grateful to all of those nearest to me, beginning with my wife and children. They have often heard the name *Kuyper* over the years, not only in my sermons, but also in our conversations around the table. Thank you for all that you mean to me. I love you, and I am proud of each one of you. Your accomplishments are significant. In addition, may the Lord bless three special people who have been a blessing to me—my father and mother and Edward. I dedicate this book to them with much love.

Introduction

ABRAHAM KUYPER—THEOLOGIAN AND POLITICIAN, professor of theology at the Free University of Amsterdam and a member of the Dutch parliament, and later prime minister of the Netherlands (1837-1920)—provided a coherent body of neo-Calvinist political thought based upon the foundation of biblical doctrine. He elaborated upon the major principles of politics and government that arise from the teaching of Scripture: the authority of God over the nations, blessing those countries that walk according to his ordinances; the fallen condition of human nature creating the need for government and the need for limits upon political authority; and the value of freedom that must be zealously guarded.

Kuyper affirmed that his political theory arose from the theology of Calvinism, even contending that the roots of neo-Calvinist thought on church and state are to be found in the political philosophy of John Calvin. It is true that Kuyper stands in continuity with many aspects of Calvin's political thought. Calvinian ideas on natural law, total depravity, social renewal, and republicanism are all repeated in Kuyper's teaching. There is, however, a sharp contrast between Calvin and Kuyper on the issues of religious liberty and church disestablishment. Calvin accepted neither position, while Kuyper was a vigorous champion of both ideas. Kuyper, in fact, looked to the American constitutional arrangement for his thinking on the relationship of church and state.

Contemporary Kuyperians at times embrace political positions on the left, even while they embrace Kuyper as one of their

INTRODUCTION

own. He was though a prototype of American conservatism. He aligned himself with the Republicans, the party of Abraham Lincoln. More than that, the constituent elements of American conservatism are reflected in his political theory.

This volume undertakes an examination of the fundamental principles of Kuyper's political thought. Chapters 1 through 3 demonstrate that Kuyper is prototypical of the main features of American conservatism in the twentieth century. Chapters 4 and 5 argue that Kuyper's position on church and state drew from the American constitutional tradition. More specifically, the current of Madisonian thought on church and state moved him in his own teaching on church-state relations. Chapters 6 and 7 show that Kuyper's neo-Calvinist political theory stands in continuity with the Calvinian tradition on the matter of the church and social reformation. These chapters also provide a specific application of how church and state are to be related in a Kuyperian perspective: the church as institution and organism has a crucial, foundational role to play in resisting tyranny and reforming the state. The argument demonstrates the ongoing relevance of Calvinistic principles to the contemporary issue of judicial tyranny in the United States.

Kuyper's political thought provides a coherent body of political theory with enduring value for the political engagement of the Christian community in our time.

I

Conservatism

THE DOMINANT CHARISMATIC FIGURE in American conservatism in the twentieth century was Ronald Reagan.¹ He burst upon the national scene on October 27, 1964 in his televised speech in support of the Republican presidential nominee Barry Goldwater. In that address, Reagan articulated the principles of political conservatism. More than that, "he stepped into history," becoming a major figure in the nation's political life.²

Reagan was larger than life, "an apostle of full blown political and economic conservatism."³ He embodied the conservative political tradition that had been affirmed by such American intellectuals as Russell Kirk and William F. Buckley.

The antipathy toward Reagan on the part of contemporary disciples of Abraham Kuyper is revealing. Today, many Kuyperians are politically liberal.⁴ The left-leaning positions of contemporary Kuyperians were reflected in the *Reformed Journal*.⁵ Readers in the 1980s would have drawn the conclusion that followers of

---

1. Kirk, *The Politics of Prudence*, 152, writes, "If, then, I am asked to declare what the typical American conservative believes in—why, he believes in Ronald Reagan and Mr. Reagan's general principles and prejudices. Mr. Reagan did not create the conservative character, of course; but he embodies it."
2. Noonan, *When Character Was King*, 87.
3. Nisbet, *Conservatism*, 102.
4. Lucas, "Southern-Fried Kuyper?," 199; Hexham, "Christian Politics," 2.
5. Jellema, "Abraham Kuyper's Answer," 10–14.

1

Kuyper despised Ronald Reagan.[6] The leftward orientation of contemporary Kuyperians is telling. It is compelling evidence of a significant departure, a drifting away from the fundamental political principles that Kuyper advocated.[7]

Kuyper was a champion of political conservatism.[8] He stood in the trajectory of core conservative principles affirmed by Ed-

6. Lucas, "Southern-Fried Kuyper?," 199 n. 44. Numerous examples of Kuyperian distaste for Reagan may be cited. Brinks, "The Unlikely Heretic," 4, asserts that Reagan needed to admit his errors regarding Iran-Contra. Boer, "So Hollow a Figure," 2-3, attacks Reagan's character and intelligence, portraying him as the laziest president ever and a man who was ignorant of history. In Boer's conception, Reagan was incapable of writing his own speeches, depending on subordinates to prepare his remarks. Reagan was merely an actor who "mastered his lines with professional finesse, but seldom mastered the issues that the lines were about" (3). Wolterstorff, "An Open Letter to Ed Ericson," 2-4, distances himself from conservatism and contends that the Reagan administration engaged in a selective morality. Beversluis, "Backwards Theology," 3-4, maintains that Reagan's supply-side economics was bad economics because it reflected a "backwards theology." Balmer, "Learning from Ivan," 5, declares that Reagan presided over a period of "predatory capitalism" and failed to provide the "vision and moral leadership" that America needed. Wells, "Kinder and Gentler," 2, rejects the foreign policy stance of the Reagan presidency, advocating the cutting of military spending and "abandoning the macho posturing of the early Reagan years and the rhetoric about 'standing tall' against an 'evil empire.'" In his article "Taking Stock of Reagan," Wells affirms that Reagan's economic policies were a failure and that Reagan's leadership was "as defensive and uncertain as" that provided by Jimmy Carter (2).

7. Bolt, "A Kuyperian Reflects," 12, distances himself from Kuyperians on the left: "When I had the privilege ... of spending a number of years probing Abraham Kuyper's own attitudes toward the United States of America, I began to realize that this was precisely the place where I no longer shared the views of many of my fellow Kuyperian neo-Calvinists on the progressive, center left. I don't think they share my enthusiasm for our country's reality." "What progressive, center-left positions have in common is their unreality." Bolt continues, "By 'unreality' I mean that both are triumphalist and perfectionist in their search for a polity that is not yet and, in Augustinian terms, cannot be achieved this side of the consummation."

8. There are conflicting views regarding how Kuyper's political theory ought to be described. Hexham, "Christian Politics," 7, insists that Kuyper "produces a political theory that is neither radical nor conservative, but which has the potential to be a Christian third way, incorporating true understandings of man's state found in both radical and conservative theories." He adds, "He does not adopt a conservative or radical stance, but creates his own view,

mund Burke and more recently by Ronald Reagan.[9] This thesis will be set forth by way of two major arguments. We shall first consider what conservatism is in terms of a general explanation. On this point, we shall see that Kuyper may be regarded as a forerunner of American conservatism. We shall then demonstrate by looking at the specifics that Kuyper's political thought is structured in continuity with the core tenets of contemporary conservatism in the United States.

In this connection, we shall consider three fundamental concerns of conservatism: its emphasis upon God and the moral

---

based on Scripture." Wood, *Going Dutch*, 140, asserts the following on the place that Kuyper occupied on the religious spectrum: "Neither was he a religious conservative. He would not accept the existing order. The opposite of this kind of religious conservatism . . . is . . . religious radicalism, the impulse to overturn existing structures and replace them with new ones, and that is the kind of radical Kuyper was." Wintle, *Pillars of Piety*, xiii, takes a different view. He makes the point that "1901 was the year in which Abraham Kuyper, the champion of the clerical parties in Dutch politics, became Minister President of the Netherlands." He contends further that "1901 makes a triumph of the forces of the clerical right in politics against the encroaching advances of progressive liberalism."

9. Kirk, *The Politics of Prudence*, 16, calls attention to the fact that "the conservative movement or body of opinion can accommodate a considerable diversity of views on a good many subjects." He points out in *The Portable Conservative Reader*, xiv, that "there exist wide variety in application" of conservative ideas "from age to age and country to country." While some scholars tend to focus exclusively upon the differences between British and American conservatives, Kirk, *The Conservative Mind*, 3, insists that it is possible to discern "the essence of British and American conservatism" and to identify the conservative "sentiment common to England and the United States." When I maintain that Kuyper stood in the trajectory of core conservative principles affirmed by Burke and Reagan, I am concurring with Kirk's judgment that there is a "consensus of the leading conservative thinkers and actors over the past two centuries" when it comes to certain "general principles" of conservatism (*The Portable Conservative Reader*, xv). Burke, Kuyper, and Reagan all reflected the mainstream emphasis of conservatives upon the reality of an enduring moral order, the necessity of limited government, and the inestimable value of freedom. As Kirk affirms in numerous discussions, these principles stand at the core of political conservatism in whatever country it happens to appear (*The Politics of Prudence*, 17–24, 147–48).

order, its stress upon the necessity of limited government, and its commitment to the value of freedom.

There is the profound recognition among conservative thinkers, including Kuyper, that God stands above the state and expects compliance with the demands of natural law. Likewise, although the state must provide order to society, it must not dominate the people, trampling them underfoot, and taking freedom from them.

Tradition and Reform

Let us now turn our attention to a general portrait of conservatism as a political philosophy, noting that Kuyper was prototypical of conservatism in America. We begin by acknowledging that political conservatism is a recent phenomenon in the long history of political thought.[10] Conservatism arose as a response to the fanaticism and utopian excesses of the French Revolution. The English word *conservative* comes from the French term *conservateur*. The *conservateur* in France wanted conditions to return to the way they were before the French Revolution.[11] He was "the guardian of the heritage of civilization and of the principles of justice."[12] The French *conservateur* in the days following the defeat of Napoleon appreciated the political ideas of the British statesman Edmund Burke who affirmed a "politics of prudence and prescription, guarding and preserving a country's institutions."[13]

It is true that conservatism appreciates tradition. Michael Oakeshott describes this aspect of conservative thought: "To be conservative, then, is to prefer the familiar to the unknown, to

---

10. Kirk, *The Portable Conservative Reader*, xi, makes this point: "As a coherent body of political thought, what we call conservatism is a modern development."

11. Sigler, *The Conservative Tradition in American Thought*, 2.

12. Kirk, *The Portable Conservative Reader*, xiii.

13. Kirk, *Edmund Burke*, 230. Burke affirmed that conservatism entails more than a commitment to safeguard a nation's institutions. "A conservative statesman is one who combines a disposition to preserve with an ability to reform" (ibid.).

prefer the tried to the untried, fact to mystery, the actual to the possible, the limited to the unbounded, the near to the distant, the sufficient to the superabundant, the convenient to the perfect, present laughter to utopian bliss."[14] This passage nicely expounds upon the conservative bent to honor the valuable insights that come to us from the past. This, however, is only one aspect of the instincts of the conservative mind.[15]

There are times when conservatives demand change and reform. They may express the desire to overturn the *status quo*, to return to an older and better tradition that has been elapsed in the state and in society.[16] Change is legitimate in conservative thinking, but it must be prudent change, "gradual and discriminatory."[17] "Sudden and slashing reforms are as perilous as sudden and slashing surgery."[18] The conservative thus has an antirevolutionary perspective on life.[19]

This then is the prevailing attitude of conservatism. In America there is great respect for our political principles as embodied in the Constitution. American conservatives believe that "they are the gifts of great men of old."[20] Thus there is the desire to maintain and defend the good things of the past. At the same time there is within the conservative soul a desire to restore the good things that have fallen by the wayside. Such a restoration is not merely a complete duplication of what has happened in the past. History moves forward in its growth and progress. Thus foundational political principles must be applied to a new time and situation.[21]

14. Oakeshott, *Rationalism in Politics*, 408.
15. Harbour, *The Foundations of Conservative Thought*, 1.
16. Kendall and Carey, "Towards a Definition of Conservatism," 410.
17. Kirk, *The Politics of Prudence*, 19.
18. Ibid., 20.
19. Harbour, *The Foundations of Conservative Thought*, 60.
20. Rossiter, *Conservatism in America*, 74.
21. An example of this would be seen in the contemporary conservative's desire to see the restoration of federalism with a renewed commitment to the principle of states' rights. Such a restoration, however, would not entail a return to the practice of slavery. Inappropriate elements from the past would fall away even while there might be a restoration of foundational constitutional principles.

An American Republican

Is it really the case that Abraham Kuyper ought to be ranked as one of the charismatic giants of political conservatism? How can this be maintained when he rejected the Dutch Conservative Party?[22] We must here keep in mind the reason for this. The Conservative Party in the Netherlands was "little more than the moderate wing of Liberalism."[23] Kuyper gave this assessment: "In every fundamental issue Conservatism and Liberalism tread the same path."[24] The Dutch Conservatives "subscribed to the same humanistic principles" as did the Liberals.[25] Kuyper was not able to support any of the political parties in the Netherlands. This was the reason for his work in the establishment of the Antirevolutionary Party.

What was Kuyper's perspective on the political situation in the United States? It was not one of total antipathy. He acknowledged in an editorial published in *The Democrat* (a Grand Rapids newspaper) on October 30, 1898, that "no true Calvinist could support" the Democratic Party, which "openly declared its sympathy to Jefferson's principles."[26] He had made the same point in his Grand Rapids Address delivered four days earlier on October 26, 1898. "The educated Hollander who is acquainted with the doctrine and principles of Jefferson cannot be a democrat," he

---

22. True conservatism and the Dutch Conservative Party would not necessarily be one and the same thing. While the Dutch Conservative Party represented a false conservatism, Kuyper, "Conservatism and Orthodoxy," 69, wanted to "rouse" the people to "the *true conservatism*." He insisted that with respect to Christianity "conservatism is so integral to the core of its being that it even refuses to abandon the human body to death but in the article concerning the 'resurrection of the body' prophecies complete salvation" (71). This is very different than "a false conservatism" that "swears by the status quo" (ibid.). Conversely, "true conservatism aims" to "preserve" the "new life" that Christ brought into the world (80).

23. Langley, "Emancipation and Apologetics," 75–76.

24. Kuyper, "Our Program," 243.

25. McGoldrick, *God's Renaissance Man*, 177.

26. This letter to the editor of *The Democrat* is found in Bolt, *A Free Church*, 483.

insisted.[27] On the other hand, he was willing to identify himself with the Republican Party. In the same speech delivered to some two thousand Dutch Americans, Kuyper announced, "If I had lived here I should be a Republican."[28] He did not, however, place his full stamp of approval on the Republican platform. He declared, "After reading the republican platform, I found that in it there is room for improvement."[29] Where was it deficient? He later specified, referring to his "regret that the Republican platform of 1896 did not openly reaffirm Hamilton's Calvinistic principles."[30]

We see then that Kuyper aligned himself in the United States with the Republican Party, the party of Abraham Lincoln, statesman of American conservatism.[31] Where did Kuyper stand with respect to Edmund Burke, the political theorist who developed the principles reflected in modern conservatism?[32] There is no question that he greatly admired Burke.[33] Kuyper referred to him as "an excellent Antirevolutionary," "an Antirevolutionary through and through."[34] In the judgment of Kuyper, Burke exemplified the political principles of the Dutch Antirevolutionary Party. Even more than that, he affirmed that Burke's political perspective had value for the Dutch Antirevolutionaries. "We Dutch Calvinists," he said, "want to be like Burke: *for* freedom but *against* the total overturning of all natural order."[35]

We find in this last statement a major constituent of political conservatism: its antipathy to radicalism, the total overturning of the natural order. Kuyper's conservative instincts were largely

---

27. The public address that Kuyper gave in Grand Rapids is also provided in Bolt, *A Free Church*, 471.
28. Ibid.
29. Ibid., 471–72.
30. Ibid., 484.
31. Belz, "Abraham Lincoln," 518.
32. Dunn and Woodard, *The Conservative Tradition in America*, 49.
33. Heslam, *Creating a Christian Worldview*, 100.
34. Kuyper, "Calvinism," 314.
35. Ibid., 315.

directed against the French Revolution.[36] He did not like the direction it took with respect to God or man. "The French Revolution," he affirmed, "ignores God. It opposes God."[37] "The French Revolution," he elaborated, was characterized by "setting God aside and by placing man on the throne of God's Omnipotence."[38] "The sovereign God" was "dethroned and man with his free will" was "placed on the vacant seat."[39] Kuyper even admitted that the name of his political party owed its origin to its antithetical response to the French Revolution. "Our Calvinists often call themselves Antirevolutionaries," he said, "over against the French Revolution's basic premise of emancipating the creature from the Creator."[40]

Antirevolutionary Reform

Like all conservatives, Kuyper objected to hasty and slashing reforms, preferring that necessary change be cautious and discriminatory.[41] As a true conservative, he wanted change in the Netherlands that restored an older political tradition, even as he updated it for his own time.[42] More specifically, he wanted to re-Christianize society.[43] He yearned for a return to the Calvinism of

36. Van Dyke, "Groen van Prinsterer," 85.
37. Kuyper, *Lectures on Calvinism*, 87.
38. Ibid., 99.
39. Ibid., 87.
40. Kuyper, "Calvinism," 284.
41. Kirk, *The Politics of Prudence*, 19–20.
42. Skillen, "Politics," 199, observes that Kuyper believed that "Calvinism had to be liberated from various unbiblical chains that still held it in check. Not the least of the bondages in which Calvinism found itself in Kuyper's day was the old Roman and medieval view of politics which did not allow for the legitimate unfolding of political life in accord with God's ordinances of public justice. The unhealthy alliance of church and state which, back in Calvin's day, had led to such things as the burning of Servetus at the hands of the Genevan government because of his heretical convictions was something from which Calvinism had to be set free."
43. Heslam, "Prophet of a Third Way," 14.

the early Dutch Republic.⁴⁴ His longing was for a revival of Dutch culture for Christ.⁴⁵ Even as Kuyper celebrated the triumphs of Calvinism in the past, he distinguished himself from "the kind of Calvinists who seek salvation in a return to the past" in total.⁴⁶ He rejected a "false conservatism" that seeks "to recall the old," an approach that seeks "to reconstruct what the hands of their ancestors had fashioned."⁴⁷ He was not a reactionary and strenuously objected to what he called "the old libel . . . that we, Dutch Calvinists, are a party of reaction!"⁴⁸ Indeed, his realization that Calvinism needed to be brought up-to-date, in line with modern society, led him to use the term *neo-Calvinism* to refer to his worldview and system of political thought.⁴⁹ It was as a neo-Calvinist political theorist that Kuyper affirmed that "sacred to the Christian statesman . . . is the struggle . . . for progress, because God's Word shows him a forward movement in the life of the nations toward a fixed goal—a movement which reactionism would retard and which stagnation would delay until it was too late."⁵⁰

The point that must be remembered is that Kuyper was not a leftist, a liberal, or a progressive in his political views. He built his political philosophy, like all conservatives do, by tapping into an older tradition—particularly the Bible and the theology of Calvinism.⁵¹ The ultimate foundation that Kuyper drew from was the

44. Harinck, "Abraham Kuyper's," 77.
45. Dennison, "Dutch Neo-Calvinism," 276.
46. Kuyper, "Calvinism," 315.
47. Kuyper, "Conservatism and Orthodoxy," 72–73.
48. Kuyper, "Calvinism," 317.
49. Heslam, *Creating a Christian Worldview*, 87–88.
50. Kuyper, "Our Program," 256.
51. Conservatives recognize that "the roots of conservative thought . . . extend deep into the history of ideas and of social institutions" (Kirk, *The Portable Conservative Reader*, xi). Kirk, for example, regarded Cicero as a conservative. Goldwater, *The Conscience of a Conservative*, xxv, likewise directed attention to the deep roots of conservatism: "The principles on which the Conservative political position is based . . . are derived from the nature of man, and from the truths that God has revealed." He added, "Circumstances do change. So do the problems that are shaped by circumstances. But the principles that govern the

biblical tradition itself.⁵² In his articulation of the Antirevolutionary program he affirmed that the Word of God sets forth enduring political principles that can be applied to contemporary political life.⁵³ These "principles of political order," "the givens of God's Word" are "eternal, valid for all nations and in force for all times."⁵⁴

Holy Scripture

What exactly did Kuyper mean by this statement? Did he embrace a theonomic position in which the contemporary state embraces

---

solution of the problems do not."

52. Since our later discussion on Kuyper's core tenets (God, the state, and human freedom) directly arises from his Calvinist theology, let us restrict ourselves at this point to his appeal to the Scripture. Kuyper's 1898 lecture on "Calvinism and Politics" at Princeton Theological Seminary is a discourse in which he unpacked the political principles that flow from Calvinist theology.

53. It would be an erroneous conclusion to maintain that Kuyper embraced a theocratic political theory, an arrangement in which the clergy governs the state. Cf., Walton, *Zwingli's Theocracy*, 1. In his *Lectures on Calvinism*, 85, he explicitly rejected theocracy as an arrangement that applied in a technical sense to ancient Israel alone. He also affirmed that the church is only "sovereign within her own domain," adding that "she has no power over those who live outside of that sphere" (108). In this respect, Kuyper stood in continuity with Calvin who rejected a theocratic arrangement in which the clergy would have direct civil authority, the kind of structure that was found in the Jewish ghettos of Europe in which the head of the community was the rabbi and the constitution was the Torah, the Talmud, and rabbinic commentaries. Cf., Graham, "Kuyper, Neo-Calvinism, and Contemporary Political Philosophy," 58. Recent developments in Iran and the short-lived Taliban experience in Afghanistan resulted in theocratic governments. There was more, however, than a full restoration of the shari'a. The scholars (the ulema) would rule directly. This was without precedent in Islamic history. Feldman, *The Fall and Rise of the Islamic State*, 135-36, observes that in Shia Iran, the supreme leaders and the Council of Guardians exercise real power. The president who is popularly elected has limited power. The Sunni Taliban attempted to do something similar in Afghanistan. Men who purported to be scholars took direct political control (138). In both countries, scholars exercised rule without a constitutional counterbalance. Despotism resulted (137-38).

54. Kuyper, "Our Program," 254-55.

the Mosaic legal code as the foundation of its laws?[55] He did not. He fully sided with the position of Calvin who declared that those who insist upon "the political system of Moses" rather than being "ruled by the common laws of nations" embrace a position that is "false and foolish."[56] Kuyper was no less adamant than Calvin in his position: "Taking Holy Scripture as a complete code of Christian law for the state, would, according to the spiritual fathers of Calvinism, be the epitome of absurdity."[57]

Kuyper thus rejected the theonomic use of the political materials in the Bible. In his judgment, Scripture provides something less than a legal codebook. "It reveals to us the ground rules," "the principles that govern man's life together."[58] What exactly did he have in mind at this point? What are the ground rules of political life?[59] The Bible, he maintained, draws attention to foundational

---

55. Vander Hart, "Abraham Kuyper," 74, observes, "Theonomists utilize the phrase 'God's law.'" Kuyper, on the other hand, preferred to use the expression "the ordinances of God."

56. Calvin, *Institutes* IV.20.14 (unless otherwise noted, all references are to the 1559 edition).

57. Kuyper, "Our Program," 248.

58. Ibid., 250.

59. John Locke also affirmed that the Bible has authority with reference to the political life of a nation. Hashemi, *Islam*, 70, calls attention to the fact that Christian Europe for over a millennium was characterized by the attempt to maintain religious uniformity. Heretics were punished, and dissent was crushed (77). Inquisitions and expulsions were the order of the day (72). Even Locke initially believed that the state had the right to regulate the public manifestation of religion in society (73). His thinking, however, changed. In his treatise *A Letter Concerning Toleration* (1689), Locke appealed to the Scripture, acknowledging its authority in political matters (82). He proceeded to build a scriptural case for religious toleration (83). He appealed to both reason and revelation in support of his view that there needed to be a separation of church and state (79). By building his argument upon the Bible, Locke was able to show that the political change he was arguing for was in keeping with Christianity (88). Toleration, Locke argued, was the true Christian position (89). Locke's religious ideas helped to move society in the direction of political secularism, a society in which there would be "twin tolerations" (129). In other words, there would be the toleration of political and religious institutions (123). Politicians would have the freedom to act apart from religious authorities. Clergy and churches would have the freedom to act apart from interference by politicians.

principles that include the reality of natural law, the need for limited government based upon the fallen nature of man, and the importance of freedom for the people.[60]

The Christian political leader, Kuyper argued, will always be "standing on firm ground in his contemplation of basic principles." "He possesses the compass that points the way across the tossing seas even when there is no land in sight."[61] He knows, in the first place, that there is the reality of natural law, a law above the law. "He is convinced that justice is not made by the statesman, but that it exists before the very notion of justice crosses his mind, and he can only approximate it in his formulation of laws."[62] He knows, secondly, that something is dreadfully wrong with human nature. There is "the reality of sin," "this awful reality."[63] This means that rulers cannot be trusted. The Christian politician insists that government must be limited. "He knows on the basis of God's Word that absolutistic rule, monarchy in an untempered sense, constantly threatens to turn into tyranny."[64] He knows, thirdly, that liberty must be guarded and maintained. "Sacred to the Christian statesman," Kuyper wrote, "is the struggle for freedom." "Scripture teaches him to view Christian people as a free people, who may not be used as an instrument but who themselves act as a living member of the body politic."[65]

We have thus far seen that Kuyper fits the general portrait of a political conservative. He opposed radicalism, even while he looked to an older political tradition, ultimately the Word of God itself. We now move in the next chapter to our second argument in support of Kuyper's conservative credentials. We shall note that three foundational concerns of contemporary conservatism stood at the heart of Kuyper's political philosophy.

60. The core principles that surface in the biblical text constitute the fundamental tenets of American conservatism.
61. Kuyper, "Our Program," 256.
62. Ibid., 255.
63. Ibid., 247.
64. Ibid., 255.
65. Ibid., 256.

2

God and Humanity

AMERICAN CONSERVATISM PLACES EMPHASIS upon the transcendent realm of God and law, and also upon the way in which such concerns relate to religion and morality. Burke and his conservative disciples down to the present day have believed in the reality of natural law. "We think it necessary," Burke maintained, "to declare that the laws of morality are the same everywhere, and that there is no action which would pass for an act of extortion, of peculation, of bribery, and of oppression in England, that is not an act of extortion, of peculation, of bribery, and oppression in Europe, Asia, Africa, and all the world over."[1] "*The conservative believes that there exists an enduring moral order.*" Furthermore, "*that order is made for man, and man is made for it.*"[2] Of course, the conservative's faith in the reality of a transcendent moral order carries a significant implication with it: "His belief in an objective, absolute, universal realm of values and standards of right and wrong is ultimately grounded in his belief in God."[3]

The belief in the reality of God and a moral order that he imposes upon humanity leads to the additional conservative emphasis upon the importance of religion and morality in the social and political order.[4] It is the position of conservatism that religion

---

1. Burke, *The Philosophy of Edmund Burke*, 17.
2. Kirk, *The Politics of Prudence*, 17; italics original.
3. Harbour, *The Foundations of Conservative Thought*, 84.
4. This was the problem that Kuyper had with the French Revolution.

is absolutely necessary for a good society.[5] "We know, and what is better we feel inwardly," Burke declared, "that religion is the basis of civil society, and the source of all good and all comfort."[6] The church, Burke affirmed, provides for society "the healing voice of Christian charity."[7] While religion lays the foundation, ethics provides the setting in which the good society is to be found.[8]

Conservatism provides compelling argumentation for the crucial importance of morality in the social order.[9] Kirk writes as follows: "A society in which men and women are governed by belief in an enduring moral order, by a strong sense of right and wrong, by personal convictions about justice and honor, will be a good society—whatever political machinery it may utilize." On the other hand, Kirk continues, "A society in which men and women are morally adrift, ignorant of norms, and intent chiefly upon gratification

---

Wolterstorff, "Abraham Kuyper," 32, makes the point that for Kuyper the French Revolution was a "great evil" because "first and foremost, it represented aggressive atheism. Kuyper believed with all his heart that we must expect something like the French Revolution to happen when political power falls into the hands of militant atheists, hostile to religion, who believe that there is no transcendent source of authority by which our actions are to be measured."

5. Harbour, *The Foundations of Conservative Thought*, 6.

6. Burke, *Reflections on the Revolution*, 109.

7. Ibid., 11.

8. Nisbet, *Conservatism*, 68, writes, "Conservatism is unique among major political ideologies in its emphasis upon church and the Judaeo-Christian morality."

9. Conservatives believe that a moral society is more important than political democracy. In fact, a pure democracy can be dangerous. Kirk, *The Conservative Mind*, 137, states, "The pure democrat is the practical atheist; ignoring the divine nature of law and the divine establishment of spiritual hierarchy." Robert Dabney, a contemporary Reformed theologian of Kuyper in America, is another conservative thinker who opposed democracy as a form of civil polity—due to his distrust of the common man. Dabney was under no illusion that the people were "the spring of innocence and virtue" (Bozeman, "Inductive and Deductive Politics," 707). Among the masses, Dabney contended in "Civic Ethics," 113, were the "foolish and morally incompetent." Such statements show Dabney's embrace of the Calvinist doctrine of total depravity and that he stood in the mainstream of Old School Presbyterianism, "the branch of the antebellum Presbyterian church that refused to acquiesce in the rising current of optimism about man and his capacities" (Bozeman, *Protestants*, 33).

of appetites, will be a bad society—no matter how many people vote and no matter how liberal its formal constitution may be."[10]

In his famous lecture on politics at Princeton Theological Seminary, Kuyper stated, "It must be shown for what fundamental political conceptions Calvinism has opened the door."[11] Calvinism, he insisted, has maintained the importance of God and natural law for the political life of a nation. Religion and ethics, he affirmed, are crucial for the prosperity of a political community. These concerns, as we have already noted, stand as core principles of political conservatism in America.

"Calvinism," Kuyper affirmed, "taught us . . . that God, in His Majesty, must flame before the eyes of every nation." The "wellbeing" of every nation is directly contingent upon whether or not "they walk after His ordinances."[12] God is the one "unto Whom the prayer of the people ever ascends, to bless our nation and, in that action, us and our house."[13] A nation by its conduct may experience the "favor of God" or "by its sin" may reach the point where it "has utterly forfeited the blessing" of God.[14]

This indeed was Kuyper's great concern with respect to the Netherlands, which in his judgment had deteriorated spiritually and morally. "The spirit of apostasy" was felt.[15] The "toxic fluid" of

10. Kirk, *The Politics of Prudence*, 17.
11. Kuyper, *Lectures on Calvinism*, 79.
12. Ibid., 81. Skillen, "Politics," 198, writes as follows regarding the views of Groen van Prinsterer and Abraham Kuyper: "True human freedom and responsibility in history, they asserted, is possible only through submission to *God's ordinances*. Human beings cannot escape the 'heteronomous' character of creaturely life. The true law of life comes from outside the human will; it comes from another—from the will of God."
13. Kuyper, *Lectures on Calvinism*, 90.
14. Ibid., 84. James Thornwell, an American Reformed theologian who lived at the same time as Kuyper, in "Sermon on National Sins," 523, took the same view. He said, "Sin has been the ruin of every Empire that ever flourished and fell." Referring to the empires of Daniel's prophecy, he added, "Assyria, Persia, Greece and Rome have paid the penalties of the Divine law." Every government, like every individual, has but two choices: "The only alternative with States, as with their subjects, is, repent or perish."
15. Kuyper, "Maranatha," 214.

the French Revolution had "seeped into nearly all" the "institutions, laws, and customs" of the Dutch Republic. It was Kuyper's burden to labor toward the reform of the religious life of the Dutch people. He held out the hope that "the possibility remains that the spirit of apostasy can be arrested."[16]

In addition to the classical conservative stress upon religion and ethics, Kuyper drew attention to the reality and importance of natural law for the political life of a nation.[17] Like Aquinas and Calvin before him, Kuyper postulated the existence of both eternal law and natural law—insisting further that human law as enacted by civil government must harmonize with them.

There are, he said, "eternal principles of right."[18] "Justice is not made by the statesman, but . . . exists before the very notion of justice crosses his mind."[19] "Eternal Right" is found "in God."[20] Natural law, which Kuyper believed in, is simply the imprinting of this eternal law upon the mind of man. He expressed his appreciation for the place of natural law in the Declaration of Independence and the fact that "the Americans asserted themselves by virtue—'of the law of nature and of nature's God.'"[21]

Kuyper manifestly rejected the views of legal positivism, which denies the reality of natural law.[22] "Calvinism protests," he asserted, "against the horrible conception that no right exists above and beyond existing laws."[23] Kuyper sided with the view of Calvin, affirming that human "law is right . . . because its contents

16. Ibid., 212.

17. VanDrunen, "Abraham Kuyper," 285, states, "Kuyper in fact bore significant similarities to his Reformed predecessors, both Calvin and Reformed orthodox figures, on matters pertaining to natural law." He "affirmed that God himself wrote his law on the heart of every person and that knowledge of this law was to play a crucial role in the development of a sound social and political life." Cf., Groen van Prinsterer, *Lectures*, 212.

18. Kuyper, *Lectures on Calvinism*, 89.

19. Kuyper, "Our Program," 255.

20. Kuyper, *Lectures on Calvinism*, 90.

21. Ibid., 86.

22. Nash, *Life's Ultimate Questions*, 186.

23. Kuyper, *Lectures on Calvinism*, 98.

are in harmony with the eternal principles of right."[24] If "the existing law" does not harmonize with "the eternal Right in God," Calvinism "creates in us the indomitable courage incessantly to protest against the unrighteousness of the law in the name of this highest Right."[25]

A Flawed Humanity

A second core principle of conservatism relates to its emphasis upon the necessity of limited government due to its deep distrust of human nature. Our consideration under this heading will proceed in the following manner. We shall take note of the fact that the existence of government is a result of the fundamentally flawed character of human nature. Order must be brought upon the chaos of human society by the strong arm of legitimate governmental authority. The problem is that government officials are themselves marred with moral defects—particularly with the vices of pride and ambition, desiring ever to expand their power and dominating others with it as they seek to impose their utopian vision upon others. The inevitable loss of freedom that this entails leads to the strong emphasis in conservatism upon the need for limits upon government. Let us now observe how the conservative tradition, along with Kuyper, follows this line of reasoning.

Foundational to the conservative political theory is its distrust of human nature. In the conservative view, humanity is morally flawed and defective.[26] "Human nature suffers irremediably from certain grave faults, the conservatives know."[27] In political liberalism, wrongdoing results form ignorance, a simple lack of knowledge regarding the difference between right and wrong. Conservatism, on the other hand, teaches that a person can know

---

24. Ibid., 89.
25. Ibid., 90.
26. Dunn and Woodard, *The Conservative Tradition*, 53.
27. Kirk, *The Politics of Prudence*, 21.

what is right and yet freely chooses to do what is wrong.[28] Government is necessary because of the chaos that is engendered by morally broken people. The authority of the state must bring order to human affairs.[29]

As a Calvinist thinker and a conservative in the tradition of Burke, Kuyper affirmed that he did not believe in "some idea of human greatness but rather in a profound sense of sin."[30] With respect to other approaches, he said, "A political theory that pays no attention to the reality of sin . . . remains stillborn; it is a rarefied abstraction that fails to take real life into account." Antirevolutionary theory stood in contrast to the views of other ideologies: "It emphasizes strongly this awful reality."[31]

Government owed its existence to this awful reality: "Calvinism has . . . placed in the foreground, as the primordial truth—*that God has instituted the magistrates, by reason of sin.*"[32] "When sin reveals itself in all manner of shame and unrighteousness—the glory of God demands that these horrors be bridled, that order return to this chaos, and that a compulsory force, from without, assert itself to make human society a possibility."[33] What would a "sinful humanity" be like "without law and government, and without ruling authority"? Kuyper admitted that it "would be a veritable hell on earth."[34] Thus "the magistrate is an instrument of

28. Harbour, *The Foundations of Conservative Thought*, 37.

29. Burke, *The Works and Correspondence*, 3:230, affirmed that order "inheres in good and steady government."

30. Kuyper, "Calvinism," 285.

31. Kuyper, "Our Program," 247.

32. Kuyper, *Lectures on Calvinism*, 79; italics original.

33. Ibid., 81–82.

34. Ibid., 81. Kuyper insisted in *Common Grace*, 104, that we as humans have by nature authority over nothing: "You have no authority over anything, no matter what it my be, unless God grants you this authority." He elaborated, "Now if this establishes that human beings have no authority, not even over an animal or tree, not even over a worm or an insect, unless God gives that authority to them, then even far less can someone set himself up as an authority in order to assume power and control over another *person*, let alone over millions of *people* at the same time. Such a power and such a control can exist only if God institutes and ordains that dominion of one *person* over other

'common grace,' to thwart all license and outrage and to shield the good against the evil."[35] In light of this, "Calvinism" has taught us an important lesson: "That we have gratefully to receive, from the hand of God, the institution of the State with its magistrates, as a means of preservation, now indeed indispensable."[36]

Pride in Politics

The problem is that sinners, human beings with deep moral deficiencies, run government, which is intended to be an instrument of common grace.[37] What is the root sin of politicians in the conservative view? Conservatives insist that the fundamental human defect is found in his pride.[38] This pride manifests itself in all radical agendas that seek to overthrow the existing order in their attempt to establish an Earthly Paradise.[39] An example of this, William Buckley reminds us, is seen in Communist dogma with its eschatological vision entailing "the elimination of poverty, war, inequality, insecurity." In a very real sense, Communism "holds out a millennial vision," and "indicates the means (revolution) of effecting this millennium."[40]

This is how human pride works itself out in the political arena. Political radicals believe that human reason has the capability of establishing a utopian order—a perfect society of justice, peace, and happiness.[41] For rationalists, "Political activity consists

---

people" (105).

35. Kuyper, *Lectures on Calvinism*, 82. Kuyper argued in *Common Grace* that government authority exists due to "common grace," which he explained as "God's gracious arrangement whereby he created order amid the chaos of a sinful world and arrested the disruptive destruction of sin" (102).

36. Kuyper, *Lectures on Calvinism*, 81.

37. Sherratt, "Rehabilitating the State," 127, notes that in Kuyper's political theory "the state" is an agency of common, not particular grace. Thus the task is to sustain creation, not to redeem it.

38. Harbour, *The Foundations of Conservative Thought*, 5.

39. Kirk, *The Politics of Prudence*, 18.

40. Buckley, *Up from Liberalism*, 145.

41. Harbour, *The Foundations of Conservative Thought*, 34.

in bringing the social, political, legal and institutional inheritance of his society before the tribunal of his intellect."[42] Radicalism becomes "the politics of perfection, and . . . the politics of uniformity."[43] "Political life is resolved into a succession of crises, each to be surmounted by the application of 'reason.'"[44] The political radical draws attention to the crisis at hand and then shows how reason resolves the problem. The solution to the problem may be then described as "the imposition of a uniform condition of perfection upon human conduct."[45]

The problem in the above scenario is that the god of reason inevitably fails to deliver what has been promised.[46] More than that, history records the sad story of the suffering inflicted by radicalism upon human society. "The ideologues who promise the perfection of man and society have converted a good part of the twentieth-century world into a terrestrial hell."[47]

There is then a dilemma. Government is necessary because men are not angels, but men who are not angels run government.

There is also another issue along these lines that conservatives stress. The conservative presidential nominee Barry Goldwater wrote about the corrupting influence of power. He contended that "the natural tendency of men who possess *some* power" is "to take unto themselves *more* power." "The tendency leads eventually

---

42. Oakeshott, *Rationalism in Politics*, 8.
43. Ibid., 9–10.
44. Ibid., 9.
45. Ibid., 10.
46. Utopians, nevertheless, are not deterred by the countless failures of the past. As Harbour points out, utopians continue to work from "an abstract set of principles" (*The Foundations of Conservative Thought*, 56). They steadfastly believe that "human reason can work out an absolute ethical and political system by which the lives of men and society should be ordered" (ibid., 57). When radicals take control of the government, they "force the political world to conform vigorously" (56). "Society can and should be reordered" in their view "according to some kind of detailed blueprint drawn up by human reason" (57).
47. Kirk, *The Politics of Prudence*, 21.

to the acquisition of *all* power."[48] "The Conservative," he added, "recognizes that the political power on which order is based is a self-aggrandizing force; that its appetite grows with eating."[49] "Throughout history," he warned, "government has proved to be the chief instrument for thwarting man's liberty."[50] This then is why conservatives have great concern over the growth of government, the expansion of Leviathan. They live in fear of the centralization of power.[51] This is why conservatives forever stress the theme of limited government.

Kuyper, as we have noted, regarded government and its ordering authority as a gift from God.[52] He affirmed that Calvinism "roundly condemned every position that was bound to lead to a devaluation of government and contempt for authority."[53] Kuyper recognized though that the "authority of government is exercised by sinful *men*, and is therefore subject to all manner of despotic

---

48. Goldwater, *The Conscience of a Conservative*, 11.
49. Ibid., 7.
50. Ibid., 10.
51. Nisbet, "The Restoration of Authority," 662, 664.
52. Kuyper rejected the contract theories that "tried to ground government authority in voluntary human action" (*Common Grace*, 99). Contract theorists maintained that a "person himself can call such an authority into being by his own free will" (ibid., 100). Kuyper provided this assessment: "Historically it could nowhere be demonstrated where that agreement [to establish government] had been made, where this contract had been concluded. It rested on pure fiction" (100–101). In the American Reformed scene, Dabney, *Systematic Theology*, 862–63, also opposed the classical contract theories that traced the origin of government to the will of man. There were differences among the various social contract theorists—thinkers such as Thomas Hobbes, John Locke, and Jean Jacques Rousseau. They all agreed, however, with the view that man once existed in a state of nature, a condition in which humans were "by nature absolutely free." Due to a number of problems, "inconveniences and mutual violences," men "entered into a compact with each other," thereby agreeing to establish government. Dabney did not rest content with the concept of a merely human origin to government. He contended that God ordained the existence of government. In "The Christian Soldier," 614, Dabney described it not only as "God's ordinance," but also "if it be just, one of his greatest temporal blessings."
53. Kuyper, "Our Program," 248.

ambitions."⁵⁴ "The power of the magistrate," he said, "may become the source . . . of a dreadful abuse of power."⁵⁵ He gave this warning: "Government is always inclined with its mechanical authority, to invade social life, to subject it and mechanically to arrange it."⁵⁶ As "the centralizing State grows more and more into a gigantic monster," the "citizen is finally powerless" over against it.⁵⁷

What happens when "a government . . . constantly grows in power, size, and influence"?⁵⁸ Such a state "actually becomes *God*, and has to decide how our life and existence shall be."⁵⁹ Kuyper like all conservatives understood that "the State may assert itself and oppress the free individual development."⁶⁰ Thus "we must ever watch against the danger which lurks, for our personal liberty, in the power of the State."⁶¹ Like the conservative political tradition, "Calvinism protests against State omnipotence."⁶² The power of the state must be limited.⁶³

54. Kuyper, *Lectures on Calvinism*, 81.

55. Ibid., 80. Thornwell set forth the same perspective in his "Sermon on National Sins." The state, as a "moral institute," he affirmed, "is certainly a subject capable of sin." A state may sin by its deficiencies or its excesses. It may do too little: "Like an individual it may sin by defect in coming short of its duty." The state may also do too much. It may sin not only by omission, but also by commission. Specifically, "it may arrogate too much." It was the federal legislature, Thornwell maintained, that "was guilty of making undue claims. Thornwell charged that the "Congress may transcend its powers." He then made what amounts to a foundational contention of the South regarding the national legislature: "Its one people, it may construe into one nation, and, unmindful of its origin, treat the sovereignties which created it as dependent provinces" (531).

56. Kuyper, *Lectures on Calvinism*, 93.

57. Kuyper, "Calvinism," 281–82.

58. Ibid., 283.

59. Kuyper, *Lectures on Calvinism*, 89.

60. Ibid., 90.

61. Ibid., 81.

62. Ibid., 98.

63. Kuyper in continuity with the conservative political tradition was non-utopian. Will there be a utopian paradise here upon the earth at the Second Coming? "When Jesus returns," will he find "a sacred state of happiness prevailing everywhere on earth?" He answered his own question with this

3

Limited Government

CONSERVATIVES STRESS THAT GOVERNMENT must be limited, for power is wielded by human beings who are morally flawed. As we reflect further upon this core principle of limited government, we shall consider two issues. We shall first examine the conservative insistence that government is to have a limited role in the life of a society. We shall then look at the conservative stress upon adhering to constitutional limits upon government and also its emphasis upon maintaining localism and independence in the social spheres.

The position that the state is to have a limited role in the social order presupposes that government is not omni-competent. This fundamental assumption underscores the stark contrast that exists between conservatism and leftist positions. Both liberalism and socialism operate on the supposition that government is able to solve virtually all problems. Goldwater put it this way: "The first principle of totalitarianism" is "that the State is competent to do all things and is limited in what it actually does only by the will of those who control the State."[1] Conservatives in contrast call attention to the incompetence and mismanagement of government when it strays beyond its intended function.

What then is the task of government in the conservative view? Here we must also sharply distinguish the conservative view

---

declaration: "We are told that a great apostasy awaits us' ("Maranatha," 211).

1. Goldwater, *The Conscience of a Conservative*, 10.

from that of liberalism and socialism. Oakeshott is helpful and perceptive at this point. Leftist politicians are people who look at society and are "provoked" by what they perceive to be "the absence of order and coherence."[2] More than that, "they feel that there ought to be something that ought to be done to convert this so-called chaos into order." They "tell us that they have seen in a dream the glorious, collisionless manner of living proper to all mankind." What then is the role of government for political thinkers on the left? "Such people appropriately understand the office of government to be the imposition upon its subjects of the condition of human circumstances of their dream." Such politicians thereby minimize the value of freedom in a society, for they are gripped by the mentality that "to govern is to turn a private dream into a public and compulsory manner of living."[3]

In contrast to the leftist approach to governance, conservatism limits the role of government to maintaining justice and peace. The office of government in conservatism is not to dictate to its subjects concerning their beliefs and activities. It is not to give these kinds of directives. The office of government rather is the specific and limited activity of ruling. A helpful analogy may be drawn from the realm of sports. "The image of the ruler is the umpire whose business is to administer the rules of the game."[4] This means that the umpire of government is to maintain the peace by protecting its citizens from foreign aggression and maintaining justice among the people—"to provide redress and means of compensation for those who suffer from others behaving in a contrary manner" and "to provide punishment for those who pursue their own interests regardless of the rules."[5]

---

2. Oakeshott, *Rationalism in Politics*, 425.
3. Ibid., 426.
4. Ibid., 427.
5. Ibid., 429. Oakeshott reminds us that there are advantages when "governing is recognized as a specific and limited activity" (429). "A government which is indifferent to 'truth' and 'error' alike, and merely pursues peace, presents no obstacle to the necessary loyalty" (430).

Kuyper in harmony with conservative principles sharply limited the role of the state.[6] What is "the reason d'être for the special sphere that emerged in the State"? Government, he maintained, "must provide for sound mutual interaction among the various spheres." The state is "not to suppress life nor to shackle freedom but to make possible the free movement of life in and for every sphere."[7] Life may be compared in Kuyper's thought to "one great machine."[8] The spheres may be likened to "cogwheels" that "engage each other." "Through that interaction emerges the rich, multifaceted multiformity of human life."[9]

"The highest duty of government," he contended, "remains therefore unchangeably that of justice." The goal of justice is pursued by means of force, the authority that has been conferred upon government by God. The coercive character of government is reflected in its "principal characteristic," which is "the right of life and death." "The magistrate bears the sword." The sword may be described as "the sword of *justice*," "the sword of *war*," and "the sword of *order*." The state has the limited responsibility of protecting the citizenry "against its enemies."[10] At the same time, government is "to defend individuals and the weak ones ... against the abuse of power of the rest."[11] In addition, the state, as it bears the sword of justice, is "to mete out corporal punishment to the criminal."[12]

Constitutional Restraints

The conservative political tradition advocates a limited role for government. It has stressed in accordance with this position

---

6. Hall, "A Response," 267, argues that "Kuyper advocated a circumscribed State" and "limited law agencies to regulating contracts, rather than ensuring economic rights."
7. Kuyper, "Sphere Sovereignty," 468.
8. Ibid., 467.
9. Ibid., 467–68.
10. Kuyper, *Lectures on Calvinism*, 93.
11. Ibid., 97.
12. Ibid., 93.

constitutionalism and its legal constraints upon governmental authority. The conservative does not trust in the benevolence of political leaders. He insists upon constitutional restrictions, which are "instruments of freedom and order."[13] The value of the Constitution, Goldwater asserted, is that it provides "a system of restraints against the natural tendency of government to expand in the direction of absolutism." In terms of the Constitution of the United States, it limits the authority of the federal government to specific, delegated powers. There is also "the reservation to the States and the people of all power not delegated." Finally, the power of the federal government is divided among three separate branches.[14]

Kuyper, like American conservatives, was a strong advocate of constitutional government. Calvinist constitutionalism meant in his view that God gave authority to government, but the Almighty also entrusted authority to the social spheres in its various subdivisions—to the father in the family, to the rich man in the field of business, to the scientist in the domain of science, to the artist in the realm of art. "Calvinism," he said, "demanded for both independence in their own sphere and regulation of the relation between both . . . *under the law*."[15] In fact, "Calvinism protests . . . against the pride of absolutism, which recognizes no constitutional rights, except as the result of princely favor."[16] Kuyper affirmed his continuity with Calvin and his commitment to "a just constitution that restrains abuse of authority, sets limits, and offers the people a natural protection against lust for power and arbitrariness."[17]

Decentralizing Authority

Conservatives insist that governmental authority be limited constitutionally. There is more to it than this, however. American

---

13. Kirk, *The Politics of Prudence*, 24.
14. Goldwater, *The Conscience of a Conservative*, 12.
15. Kuyper, *Lectures on Calvinism*, 94.
16. Ibid., 98.
17. Kuyper, "Calvinism," 310.

conservatives manifest a fear of centralization—the concentration of political power in one place, such as in the federal government.[18] The Conservative has "considerable apprehension" over political and administrative centralization.[19] On the hand, Buckley argues, political freedom has little meaning when political authority is centralized. On the national level in America, "an individual's vote on a matter of importance has about the weight of a grain of sand." On the local level, things are different. Political freedom has greater significance. Democracy as it is exercised in the town hall is the classical American example that localism increases the political freedom of the individual. The "voice" of the individual "has a discernible effect on the political determinations by which he is to live."[20]

Centralization brings less freedom. What else happens when there is distant political direction? "Real government by the consent of the governed gives way to a standardizing process hostile to freedom and dignity."[21] James Kilpatrick reflects the conservative sentiment: "That government is least evil when it is closest to the people."[22] Conversely, when government grows "steadily more

---

18. Orestes Brownson, a nineteenth-century Catholic political theorist in the United States, maintained in *The American Republic*, 2, that every nation has a special mission given to it by God. The Jews, for example, gave to us the Messiah. The Greeks contributed art and philosophy, and the Romans handed down law and jurisprudence (3). What is the special mission given by God to the United States? Brownson affirmed that its mission relates to "the dialectical union of authority and liberty"—or, as he put it, it has to do with bringing into existence a nation with "liberty and law, and law with liberty" (3). He argued that liberty in America thrives largely due to the way in which authority is divided in federalism between "two co-ordinate governments" (173). There is "the General government" and "the State governments" (163). He referred to this as "the American method of guarding against . . . undue centralism" (172). In his judgment, federalism is "the special merit of the American system" (254). He stated that the American system of federalism is "no invention of man . . . but is given us by Providence" (173).
19. Harbour, *The Foundations of Conservative Thought*, 7.
20. Buckley, *Up from Liberalism*, 153.
21. Kirk, *The Politics of Prudence*, 23.
22. Kilpatrick, *The Sovereign States*, ix.

centralized, steadily more remote from the people," it becomes "steadily more monolithic and despotic."[23]

American conservatives affirm that the need of the present day is for "dispersion, division, loosening, and localization of power."[24] There is the recognition that such a perspective has deep roots in the Calvinist political theory of Johannes Althusius and in the conservative thought of Edmund Burke.[25] More than that, regionalism and localism are enshrined in the Constitution, the principle of federalism being explicitly stated in the Tenth Amendment: "The powers not delegated to the United States by the Constitution, nor prohibited by it to the States, are reserved to the States respectively, or to the people."[26] What is needed in our day, conservatives insist, is for action by the people and by the state governments. The citizens themselves must demand strict obedience to the Tenth Amendment.[27] Furthermore, political officials in the states must "assert rightful claims to lost state power."[28]

Kuyper, like American conservatives, worried about the growth of centralized government.[29] Speaking about developments in the Netherlands, he said, "Once there was autonomy in the regions and towns." "And now?" he asked. "The State," he said,

23. Ibid., x.
24. Nisbet, "The Restoration of Authority," 652-53.
25. Ibid., 678. Bratt, *Abraham Kuyper*, 134, nicely summarizes the consociational theory of Johannes Althusius (1557-1638) in which "human society was . . . a pyramid of associations where power remained as close to the base as possible and where different functions of human life developed freely according to the purposes of that function and not at the call of another."
26. When federalism functions properly, neither the state government nor the federal government interferes with one another. Kilpatrick writes, "The State and Federal governments . . . must follow the paths of parallel lines . . . spheres, separate but touching. The idea . . . was that neither authority would encroach upon the other" (*The Sovereign States*, x).
27. Kilpatrick, *The Sovereign States*, x.
28. Goldwater, *Conscience of a Conservative*, 24.
29. One of the dangers of the French Revolution was that it "represented the destruction of civil society; the totalitarian regime of the state replaced society's multiple, dispersed loci of authority and claimed that all authority belongs ultimately to the state" (Wolterstorff, "Abraham Kuyper," 33).

"has annexed all these rights from the provinces, one after the other."[30] Cities and villages have authority over "the very necessities of life," he said. How ought the central government to relate to these spheres? "The State-government cannot impose its laws, but must reverence the innate laws of life."[31]

"We promote decentralization," Kuyper declared.[32] Article 10 of the Dutch Antirevolutionary Party Program of 1879 stated the following objective: "It is the desire that local and municipal autonomy be restored by means of decentralization, insofar as this does not conflict with the requirements of national unity nor violate the rights of individual persons."[33] The division of political power that Kuyper envisioned entailed a distribution of authority—dispersed on the local, the provincial, and the national level.[34]

Autonomous Spheres

Conservatism not only seeks to decentralize government by affirming the importance of localism, but also by stressing independence and autonomy in the social spheres.[35] The maintenance of

---

30. Kuyper, "Calvinism," 282. Kuyper also favored localism in church government. He believed in the autonomy of the local congregation, the church of the city that was governed by a consistory made up of ministers and elders (Wood, *Going Dutch*, 8–9). Local congregations could then form "bonds or federations with other local churches" (ibid., 94). Higher church courts above the congregation were "voluntary gatherings." "They might advise local congregations on various matters, but they wielded no binding power" (ibid., 71).

31. Kuyper, *Lectures on Calvinism*, 96.

32. Kuyper, "Calvinism," 315.

33. Provided in Bolt, "Abraham Kuyper and the Holland-America," 40.

34. How would such an administration apply to the matter of public transportation? "The municipalities should run the trams, the provincial authorities oversee the regional railroad lines, and the government in The Hague should administer the national rail service." How would this principle apply to education? "The municipalities should oversee public elementary education, the provinces run the public high schools, and the national government administer the state universities" (Langley, "Emancipation and Apologetics," 151).

35. Hall, "A Response," 267.

strong social institutions is a fundamental conservative idea.[36] The various spheres of society have distinctive ends. Churches, universities, families, trade unions, bar associations, newspapers, and all the other spheres have a different purpose for their existence.[37] The conservative insists that each sphere ought to be able to function with the greatest possible freedom.[38] Such social bodies should be free and autonomous without "becoming the handmaiden of legislature, law office, regulatory agency, and the courtroom."[39] What is the advantage of strong and free social institutions? Dunn and Woodard declare, "Institutions and regional associations serve as checks on the power of the central authority."[40]

Kuyper is perhaps most renowned for his emphasis upon sphere sovereignty.[41] He maintained that supreme power (sovereignty) resides in God alone.[42] God has "primordial Sovereignty," power and authority residing fundamentally in him. Authority as it exists primarily in God then "eradiates" downward upon mankind.[43] Authority is entrusted to the different social institutions—the family, business, science, art, agriculture, industry,

---

36. Dunn and Woodard, *The Conservative Tradition*, 51.

37. Mouw, *Abraham Kuyper*, 23–27, provides a good, short discussion on Kuyper's teaching on the spheres.

38. Nisbet, "The Restoration of Authority," 651.

39. Ibid., 655.

40. Dunn and Woodard, *The Conservative Tradition*, 51.

41. Skillen, "Politics, Pluralism," 201, succinctly summarizes Kuyper's teaching on sphere sovereignty: "Sphere sovereignty means nothing more sophisticated yet nothing less important than the fact that God is the only sovereign of this world and that all of his ordinances must be obeyed. Individuals are not sovereign; the state is not sovereign; the church is not sovereign. God alone is sovereign. And that God . . . calls his creatures to a host of different tasks, most of which can be fulfilled only in communities, through institutions, by means of organized societies, each having its own proper offices of authority and accountability. Thus . . . each special human community . . . is guarded by the Sovereign and granted its own subordinate sovereignty."

42. Kuyper, "Sphere Sovereignty," 466, defined sovereignty as "the authority that has the right, the duty, and the power to break and avenge all resistance to its will."

43. Kuyper, *Lectures on Calvinism*, 79.

commerce, navigation, guild, trade union, university.[44] In the case of the family, authority is "entrusted to the father."[45] In some of the spheres, authority falls upon the genius that dominates the field for centuries to come. In theology, there will be men like Lombard, Aquinas, Luther, and Calvin. In philosophy, thinkers will arise like Plato, Aristotle, and Kant.[46] The point is that each sphere has a unique end and a certain kind of authority. The university is given "scientific dominion." The academy has "art-power." The guild has "technical dominion." The trade union "rules over labor."[47] Each sphere, in summary, is "clothed" by God with a unique authority.[48]

"The state cannot legitimately assert its authority over against the father, nor a prince over against the rights of other governing bodies and the people within their spheres of competence."[49] This position was central in Kuyper's thinking.[50] All of the social institutions that he talked about constitute the realm of "rights and liberties."[51] Each sphere is autonomous.[52] "Neither the life of science nor of art, nor of agriculture, nor of industry, nor of commerce, nor of navigation, nor of the family, nor of human relationship may be coerced to suit itself to the grace of the government." The state is just one sphere among many.[53] It follows then that

---

44. In his speech "Sphere Sovereignty," Kuyper asserted that "there are in life as many spheres as there are constellations in the sky" (467).

45. Kuyper, "Our Program," 255.

46. Kuyper, *Lectures on Calvinism*, 94.

47. Ibid., 96.

48. Kuyper, "Our Program," 255.

49. Ibid.

50. In Kuyper's view, "a healthy social order requires a thick and rich civil society whose diverse loci of authority are not derived from the state but instead require the state's protection" (Wolterstorff, "Abraham Kuyper," 33).

51. Kuyper, *Lectures on Calvinism*, 98.

52. In "Sphere Sovereignty," Kuyper emphasized the autonomous character of the university: "Scholarship" must "not degenerate under the guardianship of Church or State" (476).

53. Van Til, "Abraham Kuyper," 271, observes, "For Kuyper, then, the state is not the totality of society, nor is it the only or final power in society. Instead, it is the regulative institution within society that respectfully regulates the roles

"the State may never become an octopus, which stifles the whole of life."⁵⁴ The "earthly sovereign" possesses "the power to compel obedience only in a limited sphere, a sphere bordered by other spheres in which another is sovereign and not he."⁵⁵

Kuyper maintained that the people are to resist encroachments by the government in the autonomous social spheres.⁵⁶ What did he think about "a people . . . which abandons to State Supremacy the rights of the family, or a University which abandons to it the rights of science"? Such a citizenry, he said, are "guilty before God."⁵⁷ Resistance to Leviathan is a moral duty. "The struggle for liberty is not only declared permissible, but is made a duty for each individual in his own sphere."⁵⁸

Conservatism stands out for its stress upon God and a revealed moral order.⁵⁹ It is characterized by its insistence upon

---

and authorities of other parts of the organism."

54. Kuyper, *Lectures on Calvinism*, 96. Kuyper acknowledged that the government may in certain circumstances intervene in the autonomous spheres of life. "It possesses the threefold right and duty: 1. Whenever different spheres clash, to compel mutual regard for the boundary-lines of each; 2. To defend individuals and the weaker ones, in those spheres, against of the power of the rest; and 3. To coerce all together to bear *personal* and *financial* burdens for the maintenance of the natural unity of the State." He then went on to qualify these statements: "The decision cannot, however, in these cases, *unilaterally* rest with the magistrate. The Law here has to indicate the rights of each, and the rights of citizens over their own purses must remain the invincible bulwark against the abuse of power on the part of the government" (ibid., 97). Mouw, "Some Reflections," 89-90, draws out the specifics of what would be entailed for government to intervene in the spheres.

55. Kuyper, "Sphere Sovereignty," 466.

56. Bratt, *Abraham Kuyper*, 135, writes, "For Kuyper the antidote to unitary power was not just spheres orbiting in theoretical sovereignty, but a resolute citizenry whose moral strength animates the spheres with vitality enough to resist encroachment."

57. Kuyper, *Lectures on Calvinism*, 98.

58. Ibid., 98-99.

59. In his speech inaugurating the Free University of Amsterdam, Kuyper drew an antithesis between people who accept biblical revelation and those who deny special revelation. Political implications flow from each position. "Those whose minds have no place for revelation" allow "the state" to "have unlimited rule, disposing over persons their lives, their rights, their conscience,"

limited government. The final core value that we shall consider relates to the matter of freedom of religion. The power of the state must be held in check lest it infringe upon the religious rights and liberties of the people.

---

and "even their faith." The full implications of this approach came to fruition in the Roman empire. "At last the State, embodied in Caesar, itself became God" ("Sphere Sovereignty," 466).

4

Church and State

KUYPER WAS AN ENTHUSIASTIC advocate of the American approach on church and state relations.¹ He spoke glowingly of "the American Constitution," believing that its "form of government was not solely the product of intelligence and statesmanship." He agreed with the view that it was a "gift of God."² He espoused a deep appreciation for the First Amendment and its commitment to church disestablishment and freedom of religion. He wanted the same two blessings to be further extended in the Netherlands of his own time period.³

    1. Brownson, *The American Republic*, contended that the paramount mission of the United States in world history confirmed "the realization of the true identity of the state" (3). He meant that America presents a nation in which there is a proper relationship between church and state. He affirmed that the two powers of church and state had never been placed in their normal relations until the American experiment came to fruition. "This mission of our country fully realized," he argued, was "to harmonize church and state." The American Constitution "places the two powers in their normal relation, which has hitherto never been done, because there never has been a state normally constituted" (269). In America, church and state are left each "to move freely, according to its own nature, in the sphere assigned it in the eternal order of things" (268).

    2. Kuyper, "Calvinism," 288–89.

    3. van der Kroef, "Abraham Kuyper," 321–22, writes, "In his first sermon in Amsterdam, Kuyper had given vent to his indignation that the state was still holding so much control over the internal organization of the Church, and had urged the establishment of 'a free church, free from the state, free from monetary pressure, free from bureaucratic control,' which would be possible

He believed that the roots of neo-Calvinist thought on church and state were to be found in the political philosophy of John Calvin. The argument of this chapter is that Kuyper's position on church and state—the embrace of church disestablishment and religious liberty—drew upon the American constitutional tradition. The distinctively American approach to church-state relations that came to legal fruition in the First Amendment was a major influence on Kuyper's thought. Since James Madison was perhaps the most eloquent spokesman of the American doctrine on church and state, we shall prove this argument by examining the remarkable continuity between Madison and Kuyper on this subject.[4]

A Love for America

Kuyper had a deep appreciation for numerous aspects of the way of life provided for in the Constitution of the United States. He referred, for example, to the "freedom to start an enterprise and to engage in commerce" and the "freedom for citizens to participate in public affairs." He made the point that "there is a duly responsible government, a small army, low taxation, freedom of organization, a free press" and "freedom of opinion." He even reflected upon "the judicial system" that "is quick and easy," and where "all, without exception, are equal before the law."[5]

It was Kuyper's position that "modern liberties flourish in America without restriction."[6] He was particularly enthused by the fact that "liberty of conscience," the "greatest of all human

---

only with autonomous church government within each community. And yet, he conceived of the Church as 'slave of both state and Synod.'"

4. Nagel, "Madison the Intellectual," 313, speaks of Madison as "very possibly one of the three or four seminal minds in American political thought." Loconte, "Faith and the Founding," 709, agrees with the assessment of Madison's "Memorial and Remonstrance"—that it "continues to stand, not merely through the years but through the centuries, as the most powerful defense of religious liberty ever written in America."

5. Kuyper, "Calvinism," 286.
6. Ibid.

liberties," was found in the United States.⁷ More broadly speaking, Kuyper positioned himself in full continuity with the First Amendment position regarding church and state: "Congress shall make no law respecting an establishment of religion, or prohibiting the free exercise thereof."⁸ He expressed his appreciation for the fact that "as regards American life, all uncertainty in this respect is removed by what" the "Constitution at first declared . . . concerning the liberty of worship and the coordination of Church and State."⁹

Kuyper's agreement with the perspective of the First Amendment is seen in his declaration of the political philosophy of the Antirevolutionary Party.¹⁰ We here find total continuity with American law: "Positive government action in matters pertaining to our *spiritual* life is something we do not desire but fundamentally oppose." "The gospel," he said, "spurns the crutches of the powerful." He added, "All it asks is unlimited freedom to develop in accordance with its own genius in the heart of our national life."¹¹ These indeed were the two things that Kuyper admired about the American position on "the separation of church and state."¹²

---

7. Kuyper, *Lectures on Calvinism*, 108.

8. Kuyper expressed his appreciation for the idea of separate spheres for church and state. "Neither the Cœsaropapy of the Czar of Russia; nor the subjection of the State to the Church, taught by Rome" is acceptable. "Only the system of a free Church, in a free State, may be honored from a Calvinist standpoint" (*Lectures on Calvinism*, 106). Kuyper's commitment to what he called "a free Church" meant that he was opposed to the idea of the "intervention of the government in the matter of religion."

9. Ibid., 99.

10. Bratt, *Abraham Kuyper*, 144, summarizes Kuyper's thinking: "The *church* grew out of the principle of grace as the first fruits of a new, redeemed humanity on earth. It was defined by the preaching of the Word and administration of the sacraments, the purity of which neither state nor any other institution was competent to judge. The church should thus be entirely free of government subsidy or regulation at the same time that it foreswore any 'right to establish political principles that would bind the state.'"

11. Kuyper, "Maranatha," 224.

12. Kuyper, "Calvinism," 290.

Church and State

Church-state separation in America, he acknowledged, was "far stricter than in Europe but proceeds from a different principle—not from the desire to be liberated from the church but from the realization that the well-being of the church and the progress of Christianity demand it."[13] Kuyper here expressed his commitment to church disestablishment as it is provided for in the First Amendment. He then went on to describe the implications of the freedom of religion clause: "This separation does not prevent sessions of Congress, political conventions and meetings from being opened with prayer. The Sabbath rest is totally respected in America, days of prayer and thanksgiving are declared by the cabinet in Washington, and every important state document makes mention of the almighty God in plain English with the reverence and devotion due from the creature to the Creator."[14]

Kuyper admired the American constitutional and religious arrangement.[15] On the one hand, the church in the United States was free from the constraints of a Constantinian state-church alliance.[16] At the same time, however, he noted that "the population of the United States" was "decidedly religious." In fact, Kuyper concluded, it was "Christian in a way we tend to call orthodox." The "orthodoxy" was "so powerful and dominant that most of the immigrants who arrive as unbelievers and unchurched take over America's supernatural life-concept in very short order."[17] "The

---

13. Ibid., 290–91.

14. Ibid., 291. Cf., West, "Religious Liberty," 5.

15. In his *Dictaten dogmatiek*, Kuyper praised the American doctrine of "separation of church and state." He noted that church-state separation did not mean the separation of religion and politics. "Magistrates are God-fearing, by proclaiming days of public thanksgiving, honoring public prayer, observing the Sabbath Day." He went on to say that separation of church and state means that "churches are entirely free" from the interference of the state in teaching, liturgy, and polity of the churches. In addition, the state, he said, did not "subsidize the churches" (quoted in Witte, "The Biography," 245).

16. Bolt, "Abraham Kuyper and the Holland-America," 50.

17. Kuyper, "Calvinism," 289–90.

people of the Union," he declared, "bear a clear-cut Christian stamp more than any other nation on earth."[18]

A Paradigm for Reform

Why did Kuyper—a *European* Reformed theologian and a *Dutch* politician—have such an intense interest in the *American* experiment in religion and politics, and their inter-relationship? Why was it the case that the new republic of the United States gripped Kuyper's heart more than old Europe?[19] What was the reason for the fact that Kuyper demonstrated an intense interest in American affairs?[20] Kuyper viewed America as the model of what he hoped to achieve in the Netherlands.[21]

Kuyper believed that the Netherlands had deteriorated both politically and spiritually. "Liberty for Dutch citizens," in his judgment, "had been significantly curtailed."[22] Furthermore, "the spirit of apostasy" was felt in his country.[23] The "toxic fluid" of the

---

18. Ibid., 289. In his 1898 visit to New York City, Kuyper, in *Kuyper in America*, 13, wrote about his impression of life in America: "The beauty of life here is: strength through self-confidence, which gives a person inner peace." He added, "And yet peaceful, far more than in Paris or London. Everything is also healthier and more ethical. There is also vice of course, but [it is] more latent. The aspect of life is purer."

19. Kasteel, *Abraham Kuyper*, 289.

20. Heslam, *Creating a Christian Worldview*, 15.

21. Bolt, "Abraham Kuyper and the Holland-America," 50. It is quite clear from Kuyper's *Grand Rapids Address* in 1898 that he viewed America as the model of what he hoped to achieve in the Netherlands. The *Grand Rapids Herald* (October 29, 1898) gives this record of his speech: "Here in this country I have read of generals and admirals assembling their crews for prayer on the eve of battle and next month you will be called for thanksgiving. Oh! were it thus on the other side." Having expressed his appreciation for American spirituality and his longing for the same thing in the Netherlands, he then declared, "Men and brethren, I see a better day dawning for my fatherland. To this end I am working." It is clear that America was the paradigm for what he hoped to achieve. See appendix C in Bolt, *A Free Church*, 472.

22. Bolt, *A Free Church*, 59.

23. Kuyper, "Maranatha," 214.

French Revolution had "seeped into nearly all" the "institutions, laws, and customs" of his Dutch homeland.[24] It was the intention of Kuyper to work toward the reform of both the political and the religious life of the Dutch people.[25] He expressed the platform of the Antirevolutionary Party in these words: "In the civil state all the citizens of the Netherlands must have equal rights before the law. The time *must* come when it will be considered inconceivable, even ridiculous, to discriminate against or offend anyone, whoever it may be, for his convictions as a Seceder or Doleant, as a Catholic or Jew."[26] Kuyper, however, longed for more than political reform. He held out hope that "the possibility remains that the spirit of apostasy can be arrested."[27] He thus exhorted his followers: "Your concern must be . . . for the salvation of your country. You must be driven by a quiet passion to throw up a dam against the rising influence of the anti-Christian principle."[28]

24. Ibid., 212.

25. In *De Zegen des Heeren,* Kuyper expressed his commitment to a pure church that would then be able to engage society in a positive way: "Only where that Church as institute stands pure again, can she also act as organism, again shining light, enlivening, preserving" (quoted in Wood, *Going Dutch,* 163).

26. Kuyper, "Maranatha," 221. Kuyper's vision of a religiously pluralistic society included a provision for anti-Trinitarians (the Jews). This went beyond the vision of the American Puritan theologian Cotton Mather who presented a commitment to a society in which toleration would be granted to all Protestants: "And Calvinists with Lutherans, Presbyterians with Episcopalians, Pedo-baptists with Anabaptists, beholding one another to fear God, and work Righteousness, do with delight sit down together at the same Table of the Lord; nor do they hurt one another in the Holy Mountain" (quoted in Miller, *The New England Mind,* 168).

27. Kuyper, "Maranatha," 214.

28. Ibid., 213. Heslam, *Creating a Christian Worldview,* draws attention to Kuyper's insistence that it was the church, not as an institution, but as an organism that was to be the agent of social renewal. For Kuyper, "the church as organism" was "the true essence of the church." What was the church as organism? It "encompassed the whole of regenerate human life" (133). The broad task of "the church as organism . . . was the transformation of human society by bringing it into harmony with the insights provided by the Christian faith" (134). In this respect, Kuyper stood in continuity with Calvin who looked, as Niebuhr affirms, *Christ and Culture,* 217, for the present permeation of all life by the gospel. As Graham describes Calvin's relationship to the world, *The*

The Dutch Republic

We have thus far reflected upon Kuyper's admiration for the American constitutional determination for church disestablishment on the national level and the accompanying right of freedom of religion. How did he explain the origin of the American Republic and its legal commitment to disestablishment and religious liberty? Kuyper linked the American constitution with the Dutch Republic of the seventeenth century, insisting that it "served as a model for the American state, more so than any British models."[29] During his American tour of 1898, Kuyper made the claim that "American institutions were of Dutch warp, although of English woof." "It was after the old Dutch republic," he argued, "that they were patterned."[30]

There is no question that it was "in the Calvinistic Netherlands," as Kuyper put it, that "all those who were persecuted for religion's sake, found a harbor of refuge." He then specified that the Jews, Lutherans, Mennonites, Arminians, Roman Catholics, and the Independents were welcomed among the Dutch.[31] In terms of the seventeenth century, it may well be the case, as Kuyper put it, that "it may be said that the Union of our seven provinces was the most advanced on this point."[32] But to affirm that the Dutch Republic was the dominant factor behind the American constitution may be saying too much. Here we must keep in mind that even Kuyper essentially admitted that the First Amendment principles concerning church and state were not fully operational in the

---

Constructive Revolutionary, 198, Calvin "did his utmost to leash it to the Word of God." Schreiner, *The Theater of His Glory*, 107, adds, "Calvin believed God was reclaiming ... history ... The renewal or 'reconstitution' of which he spoke included the renovation of society and the historical order." As to the place of the church in such a renovation, Schreiner writes, "Instead of positing a church that stood in isolation from a threatening world, Calvin saw the church as the organ that led the renewal of ... society."

29. Heslam, *Creating a Christian Worldview*, 68.
30. Ibid., 70.
31. Kuyper, *Lectures on Calvinism*, 101–2.
32. Kuyper, "Calvinism," 294.

Dutch Republic. The Netherlands had had an established church, and the implication of this was that there was not full religious liberty.[33] He stated, "The state church ruled supreme. People with other opinions might be tolerated, but the principle of religious freedom was not done justice."[34] Furthermore, the kind of freedom granted by toleration was not extensive. "There was even freedom of worship for deviating sects," Kuyper concluded. He then gave this qualification: "Albeit in private, clandestine churches."[35]

John Calvin

A related question must necessarily be raised at this point. What are the roots of Kuyper's own neo-Calvinist political thought with his firm rejection of church establishment and his embrace of religious liberty for all? Kuyper, of course, traced the doctrine of religious liberty back to Calvin himself.[36] The true nature of Cal-

33. In 1816 King William I brought church affairs under further regulation of the state, creating the Netherlands Reformed Church (NHK). "He introduced a hierarchical system of church courts with the synod at the top" (Wood, *Going Dutch*, 9). Kuyper maintained that "foisting a synodical hierarchy on the church" led to "oppression." "Christian freedom found expression in the church in the office of believers, but the synodical hierarchy disempowered this office. Instead, the synod was a yoke on believers. Kuyper urged his people to embrace liberation and the casting off of the yoke of oppression" (ibid., 103). The actions of William I reflected the Byzantine perspective on church-state relations. Witte, *Religion*, 5, notes that the "Roman emperors and their delegates convoked and presided over the major church councils, appointed and removed bishops and other clergy, and chartered and administered churches and monasteries. Numerous imperial laws regulated the internal activities of the church, the lives of its clerics and monks, the acquisition and disposition of church property, and the definition of church doctrine and liturgy."

34. Kuyper, "Calvinism," 294.

35. Ibid.

36. Calvin accepted the idea of a holy commonwealth, which precluded any commitment to freedom of religion for groups that may have dissented from the prevailing orthodoxy. The Geneva church was not a gathered-assembly model—similar to proposals made by the Anabaptists of the same time period, in which the church is a distinct entity in the midst of a larger society. In Geneva, there was a complete identification between church and

vin's thinking on this subject, he contended, could be discerned by examining those countries where Calvin's teaching spread. He thus stated, "It cannot be denied that Calvinism itself *has* ruptured the unity of the Church, and that in Calvinist countries a rich variety of all manner of church-formations revealed itself."[37] He added, "The free churches have exclusively flourished in those countries which were touched by the breadth of Calvinism, *i.e.*, in Switzerland, the Netherlands, England, Scotland, and the United States of North America."[38]

A major problem in Kuyper's thesis at this point is found in Massachusetts Bay—a seventeenth-century bastion of Calvinist doctrine and a colony that firmly rejected religious liberty. Even Increase Mather, a major Calvinist theologian of the colony, had to admit that the record of Puritan New England had some blemishes with respect to the issue of religious toleration. "In some matters relating to Conscience and difference of opinion," he said, "they have been more rigid and severe than the Primitive Christians or the Gospel doth allow."[39]

Kuyper himself even had to admit that his attempt to root neo-Calvinist thought on church and state in Calvin appeared to be problematic. His position had its difficulties, and he referred to a major one. "The difficulty of the problem," he said, "lies in the pile and fagots of Servetus."[40] Kuyper, nevertheless, persisted in trying to find the seeds of liberty of conscience in Calvin by referring to "his open recognition of the Lutheran church" and Calvin's affirmation that there may be a "departure from Christian truth" that is "a slight one, which had better be left alone." Calvin's position that "deviations on minor matters had to be tolerated"

---

society. Since Calvin held to a territorial church model all the inhabitants of the Republic of Geneva necessarily belonged to the church—a church with a Reformed confession and liturgy. People who desired the freedom to practice another religion had to go elsewhere to do so.

37. Kuyper, *Lectures on Calvinism*, 101.
38. Ibid.
39. Quoted in Miller, *The New England Mind*, 166.
40. Kuyper, *Lectures on Calvinism*, 99.

was the opening that Kuyper needed to press his claim that the American constitutional arrangement on church and state is to be traced back to Calvin. "In America," he contended, "the logical conclusion is drawn of giving freedom to all forms of worship and each individual conscience."[41]

There is no question that the American constitutional doctrine of separation of church and state has an element of continuity with Calvin's teaching. Calvin did believe in a separation of church and state in terms of their respective jurisdictions.[42] He embraced the position that there are two spheres—the civil and the ecclesiastical, the church having control over Christian discipline.[43] The two-sphere doctrine meant that Calvin and the other pastors in Geneva would have no political authority.[44] Whatever power they had would be restricted to the ecclesiastical sphere alone. Far from

---

41. Kuyper, "Calvinism," 304-5.

42. Witte, *Religion*, 23. Calvin's two-sphere doctrine was essentially the Gelasian theory. Pope Gelasius I (492-496) in *The Bond of Anathema* had maintained that "the role of kings" and "that of priests" were different. "Christ," he said, "has made a distinction between the two roles, assigning each its sphere of operation." The ministry of "priests" related to "eternal life." The focus of "imperial government" is upon "historical existence" (quoted in O'Donovan and O'Donovan, *From Irenaeus to Grotius*, 178-79).

43. Lewis, *The Crisis of Islam*, 5-7, defines Islam by contrasting it with Christianity. He does this by largely focusing upon the issue of church and state. Christianity, Lewis contends, recognized two authorities from the beginning—God and Caesar, as it were. Church and state were regarded as two different institutions dealing with different matters. Each one had a different jurisdiction. Islam, conversely, began with a religious figure (Muhammad) who was also the head of the state. He waged war, commanded armies, collected taxes, and dispensed justice. In contrast with medieval Europe which had a pope and a German emperor with different jurisdictions, Muhammad fused the two different spheres of authority in his own person—ruling over the religious and temporal affairs of his community, the *umma*.

44. It is true that the moral influence of the Geneva pastors was enormous. Social renewal was the outcome. Indirect power, however, must not be confused with a theocratic government. Spitz, *The Protestant Reformation*, 221, properly states that the power of Calvin and his ministerial colleagues was "indirect and depended upon persuasion rather than upon political office and personal tyranny." Indeed, "it is a mistake to refer to this period as one of theocratic rule."

establishing a theocracy in which Calvin and the ministers ruled the city, Calvin and his colleagues had to struggle continually to maintain the autonomy of the church over against the authority of the civil government in Geneva.[45]

The concept of church-state separation in Calvin, however, did not mean—as it did for Kuyper—that he was opposed to church establishment. Calvin did believe in the legitimacy of the state providing financial support for the church.[46] He himself was initially retained by the government in Geneva to be a biblical teacher.[47] Furthermore, contrary to Kuyper—who looked hard to find the seeds of religious liberty in Calvin—we must honestly acknowledge that Calvin was not an advocate of freedom of religion. He, in fact, stood in continuity with the medieval tradition at this point. He believed that the law of God demanded "capital punishment" for "the authors of apostasy, and so who pluck up religion by the roots."[48] He expressed his belief that the state must punish heretics within a Christian commonwealth.[49] "In a well-established

---

45. Cottret, *Calvin*, 159, 164. The Councils in Geneva reflected the influence of the Byzantine approach to church-state relations. In the East the emperor was viewed as both king and priest. It is interesting to consider the "priestly activity" of Justinian as it appears in selections from the *Corpus iuris civilis*. There is his remarkable statement about how he as the emperor intended to provide for his subjects. In *Codex* I.5.18, he said, "We have made it the chief and first object of our most urgent consideration how their souls may be saved" (191). Practically speaking, this meant that he as the emperor would give attention to the matter, as it is put in *Novella* 6, of "the true doctrine of God and the integrity of priests" (194). *Codex* I.5.18 indicates that the emperor would take "vigorous measures" to eliminate "various heresies" throughout the empire. With respect to this issue, he would not allow heretics to "summon a public assembly for irreligious and contemptible discourse and practice" (191). The quotations from Justinian are found in O'Donovan and O'Donovan, *From Irenaeus to Grotius*.

46. Kingdon, "The Political Resistance," 226, makes the point that Calvinist writers of the sixteenth century affirmed that "the prime duty of all government" is "the maintenance of the 'true' religion."

47. McGrath, *A Life of John Calvin*, 96; Wallace, *Calvin*, 16.

48. Calvin, *Commentaries on the Last Four Books of Moses*, 74-75.

49. Dabney, like Kuyper, had a problem with the classical Reformed position regarding the treatment of heretics. In his *Systematic Theology* he asserted,

Church and State

polity," he affirmed, "profane men are by no means to be tolerated, by whom religion is subverted."[50] This was why Calvin concurred with the judgment of the state in the case of Michael Servetus.[51]

James Madison

If Calvin then is not the progenitor of Kuyperian thought on church-state matters, where shall we look for the trajectory of the neo-Calvinist doctrine of church disestablishment and freedom of religion? This chapter argues that we need not look any further than the swift and deep current of the political thought of the American Founders on the subject of church and state.[52] The teaching of the Framers on church and state is well represented in the thought of James Madison, the Father of the Constitution and the principal architect of the First Amendment clauses on religion.[53] In reality, Kuyper stood in continuity with Madison, rather than Calvin, on this subject.

"Penalties have no relevancy whatever to beget belief. Evidence begets conviction; not fear and pain" (876–77). As to the issue of the religious heretic who is a law-abiding and peaceful citizen, Dabney offered this consideration to give pause to the religious persecutor: "Moral, merciful, peaceful men" are "punished with the pains due to the most atrocious crimes, because they do not take arguments in a certain way" (878).

50. Calvin, *Commentaries on the Last Four Books of* Moses, 75.

51. On October 26, 1553, the Spanish heretic Michael Servetus was put to death by the civil magistrates in Geneva. Calvin had asked that Servetus be spared the agony of being burned to death, urging the Small Council to use the more humane method of beheading. The government refused this request. See Parker, *John Calvin*, 145.

52. This swift and deep current of American political thought also impacted American Presbyterians. Noll, "What Has Been?," 9, writes about "Presbyterian accommodation to the radical new idea that church and state should be separated," reflected in the revision to Article 23 (Of the Civil Magistrate) of the *Westminster Confession of Faith*. The new paragraph stated that governments were to do "nothing positive for the churches except to ensure that all "ecclesiastical persons" enjoyed "full, free, and unquestioned liberty."

53. Howard, "James Madison," 28, affirms, "The thirty-six-year-old Madison was the dominating spirit of the Philadelphia convention." Ketcham, *James Madison*, 229, adds, "In attending to every detail of this structure, and in being

It should almost be axiomatic that neo-Calvinist thought on church and state connects with the American Founders rather than with Calvin or the Dutch Republic of the seventeenth century, or even with any other political arrangements of Kuyper's own time. The American system on church and state "secures full liberty of religious thought, speech, and action," and it provides for an arrangement in which "religion is voluntary, and cannot, and ought not to be forced."[54] It was this constitutional arrangement that Kuyper wholeheartedly supported. The point that needs to be appreciated is that such a church-state relationship was found neither in sixteenth-century Geneva, nor in the Dutch Republic of the seventeenth century. As Philip Schaff observed, "The American relationship of church and state differs from all previous relationships in Europe and in the colonial period of our history."[55]

Furthermore, there was no country in Kuyper's own time that could have been the source of his thinking on church and state. Robert Dabney, an American Reformed theologian and a contemporary of Kuyper, commented on the fact that the church-state structure of the Constitution was uniquely American: "The separation and independence of Church and State was not only not the doctrine of the Reformation. No Christian nation holds it to this day, except ours."[56] Samuel Hill aptly comments, "In the final analysis the American disestablishment of religion and the adoption of the principle of voluntarism are the qualities which have set off our nation's religious life from that of comparable societies."[57]

---

sensitive at every point to the effect of blending the various parts, Madison played his most critical role, and earned the title later bestowed upon him, Father of the Constitution." On the more narrow issue of the constitutional arrangement of church and state in the United States, Pfeffer, "Madison's," 306, declares, "A good case can be made for the premise that no single American contributed as much as, and certainly none more than, Madison to this nation's making church-state separation a fundamental, constitutionally protected principle." Cf., Labunski, *James Madison*, 223–24; Wills, *James Madison*, 164.

54. Schaff, "Church and State," 147.
55. Ibid., 148.
56. Dabney, *Systematic Theology*, 880.
57. Hill, *The South and North*, 1. Handy, "The Magna Charta," 301, puts

All of these considerations point to the American Constitution and the church-state doctrine of the Founders as being a major influence on Kuyper's thought on this subject.[58] In further support of this argument, we shall consider in the next chapter some of the noteworthy and striking continuities between Madisonian and Kuyperian thought on church and state. We shall reflect upon Madison's core principles—which "set forth the general understandings of the age"—and we shall note that it is patently evident that Kuyper had drunk deeply from the fountain of American political thought on this subject.[59] I am not arguing that Kuyper had directly studied the writings of Madison on church and state. He had, however, been impacted by the current of Madisonian thought on church and state, the perspectives of the Founders that were embodied in the First Amendment clauses on religion.[60]

---

things in perspective with his declaration that the relationship of church and state in the United States is "the first example in history of a government deliberately depriving itself of legislative control over religion." He writes, "The tradition of establishment, which had begun with Constantine . . . was being given up in America."

58. It is true that Roger Williams had established a colony in Rhode Island in the seventeenth century in which there was a commitment to church disestablishment and religious liberty. Davis, *On Religious Liberty*, 1, draws attention to the fact that Roger Williams went beyond John Locke: "In contrast to John Locke, Williams argued not just for toleration but for liberty; he recognized that religious freedom must be understood as a fundamental human right and not legislative discretion." Davis also insists that Williams stands behind the First Amendment: "Roger Williams reminds us that the American doctrine of religious liberty is not inherited from Enlightenment rationalism alone, but is equally indebted to the religious foundations of American culture" (3). Although it is probably the case that church-state relations in Rhode Island had some influence in structuring the First Amendment, there is no evidence that Kuyper was a student of Roger Williams, or that he was influenced by the constitutional arrangement of Rhode Island. On the other hand, in Kuyper's discussions of church-state relations, he frequently directed his attention to the First Amendment of the United States of America.

59. Banning, "James Madison," 118.

60. This chapter assumes that it is legitimate to work with Novak's statement, "The Wisdom of Madison," 301, that the new American order, which "separated the state from the church" and made it "independent of political control," had Madison as its "chief articulator." To put it in another way, as

5

Madisonian

WHAT THEN ARE THE core principles of Madison and Kuyper on religion and politics? We begin with their commitment to the inalienable right of people to worship God in accordance with their own conscience.

Freedom of Religion

Madison first publicly set forth his conviction regarding this right at the age of twenty-five at the Virginia Convention that convened in Williamsburg in 1776 producing the Virginia Bill of Rights. The committee that drafted Article XVI was chaired by George Mason who initially presented a statement on religious toleration. Madison offered an amendment that was incorporated into Article XVI that went beyond the mere idea of toleration to the greater fundamental right of religious liberty.[1] The clause that was included in Article XVI, which was Madison's contribution, was this: "All men

---

Drakeman contends, "Religion and the Republic," 427, Madison was the epitome of the whole of the First Amendment tradition.

1. Riemer, "Madison," 38. Thomas Paine provided a memorable portrait of the difference between religious toleration and religious liberty: "Toleration is not the opposite of intolerance, but it is the counterfeit of it. Both are despotisms. The one assumes to itself the right of withholding liberty of conscience, the other of granting it. The one is the pope armed with fire and faggot, the other is the pope selling or granting indulgences" (quoted in Ketcham, "James Madison and Religion," 81.

are equally entitled to the free exercise of religion, according to the dictates of conscience."[2] The position that is taken in this declaration is that religion must be freely exercised. Conscience alone has authority in this realm.[3] Furthermore, the freedom to discharge one's religious duties in accordance with conscience is an entitlement.[4] "All men are equally entitled" to this in the judgment of Madison.

In his "Memorial and Remonstrance" of 1785, Madison went on to elaborate further upon the idea of an entitlement, introducing the concept of freedom of religion as being an "unalienable right."[5] Once again, he highlighted the authority of the conscience in the realm of religion, the arena in which we "render to the creator . . . homage": "The Religion, then, of every man must be left to the conviction and conscience of every man; and it is the right of every man to exercise it as these may dictate."[6]

In continuity with Madison, Kuyper insisted upon the authority of the conscience when it comes to the religious life of man. "A liberty of conscience," he elaborated, "which enables every man to serve God *according to his own conviction and the dictates of his own heart*."[7] Even more striking, Kuyper affirmed that religious liberty is an inalienable right. "Each and every citizen" must be allowed by the government to have "liberty of conscience, as the primordial and inalienable right of all men."[8] He likewise demonstrated his familiarity with the place of this expression

2. Frohnen, *The American Republic*, 158.
3. Conser, *Church and Confession*, 219.
4. The concept of religious liberty as an entitlement or an inalienable right actually appeared in 1690 in Cotton Mather. "For every man to worship God according to his Conviction," Mather said, "is an Essential Right of Human Nature" (quoted in Miller, *The New England Mind*, 165). This is a strong statement for a theologian who labored in a society that had not been committed to the doctrine of religious toleration, let alone regarding religious liberty as an inalienable right. Cf., Little, "Religious Liberty," 249-70.
5. Madison, "Memorial and Remonstrance," 64.
6. Ibid.
7. Kuyper, *Lectures on Calvinism*, 109.
8. Ibid., 108.

concerning inalienable rights in American political discourse by appealing to the Declaration of Independence and its position that the Americans had acted in their relations with the British "as endowed by their Creator with certain unalienable rights."[9]

What was the Calvinian position on civil government and religion? Calvin operated on the assumption that the government has the right to proscribe and prescribe the religious life of the members of civil society.[10] Government "prevents idolatry, sacrilege against God's name, blasphemies against his truth, and other public offenses against religion from arising and spreading among the people." "It provides that a public manifestation of religion may exist among Christians."[11]

Calvin, as we have seen, believed that it is appropriate for the government to move against an anti-Trinitarian (Servetus). Madison and Kuyper with their belief in religious liberty strongly disapproved of such an action on the part of the state. Madison stated that the government is responsible for "protecting every citizen in the enjoyment of his Religion, with the same equal hand which protects his person and his property; by neither invading the equal rights of any sect, nor suffering any sect to invade those of another."[12] Kuyper also wanted government to treat all of its citizens with an equal hand. "In the state," he insisted, "all citizens of the Netherlands must have equal rights before the law." He maintained that it is "ridiculous, to discriminate against or offend anyone, whoever it may be for his convictions." He specifically

---

9. Ibid., 86.

10. Kuyper believed that there was a problem with the view that the state should help the church to enforce right belief. In his *Tractaat van de Reformatie der Kerken*, Kuyper asserted that "this proposition supposes that the magistrate is in a position to judge the difference between truth and heresy, an office of grace which, as appears from the history of eighteen centuries, has *not* been granted by the Holy Spirit, but *withheld*" (quoted in Wood, *Going Dutch*, 111). Brownson, *The American Republic*, 269, made a similar point, commenting that "the emperors, inheriting the old pontifical power, could never be made to understand their own incompetency in spirituals, and persisted to the last in treating the church as a civil institution under their supervision and control."

11. Calvin, *Institutes* IV.20.3.

12. Madison, "Memorial and Remonstrance," 66.

stated that he opposed discrimination against the Jews, who are, of course, anti-Trinitarians.¹³ The most that the true church can do with respect to other religious groups, he said, is to "fight against these her spiritual battle." The weapons employed in such a battle are "spiritual."¹⁴

In contrast with the Calvinian or the Byzantine model, Madison and Kuyper rejected the assumption that government has any jurisdiction over the religious lives of the people. The Byzantine arrangement is exemplified in the perspective of Justinian. "In providing for our subjects' every advantage," he declared, "we have made it the chief and first objective of our most urgent consideration . . . how all persons may revere the orthodox faith with sincere intention." He then stated, "And finding many astray in various heresies, we have taken vigorous measures . . . to change their minds for the better."¹⁵ Although Calvin rejected the Erastian structure in the Reformed community in Zurich, he nevertheless agreed that government has a certain jurisdiction over the

13. Kuyper, "Maranatha," 21.

14. Kuyper, *Lectures on Calvinism*, 106. Kuyper liked to draw attention to the history of the Netherlands, which became "a harbor of refuge" for all kinds of religious groups—Jews, Lutherans, Mennonites, Arminians, Roman Catholics, and Independents (*Lectures on Calvinism*, 101-2). It was Madison who called attention to the advantage of religious pluralism; he affirmed that it was the necessary bulwark that could guarantee freedom of religion. In a speech before the Virginia Convention of 1788, Madison explained why there is freedom of religion in the United States. He argued that such freedom was due to the existence of many different religions: "If there were a majority of one sect, a bill of rights would be a poor protection for liberty. Happily for the [United States] they enjoy the utmost freedom of religion. This freedom arises from the multiplicity of sects, which pervades America, and which is the best and only security for religious liberty in any society. For where there is such a variety of sects, there cannot be a majority of any one sect to oppress and persecute the rest" (quoted in Hunt, *Life of James Madison*, 176). Emmerich, "The Enigma of James Madison," 55, draws attention to Madison's political realism: "He was a political realist who realized that 'paper proclamations' alone could not guarantee a society committed to religious liberty." Riemer, "Madison," adds, "The value of a multiplicity of religious sects for the preservation of religious liberty was a theme Madison grasped early" (43).

15. *Codex* I.5.18. Quoted in O'Donovan and O'Donovan, *From Irenaeus to Grotius*, 191.

religious thoughts and practices of citizens. The concern of the magistrate, Calvin argued, "extends to both Tables of the Law."[16] Indeed, the intensity of Calvin's conviction at this point is reflected in his reference to "the folly of those who would neglect the concern for God and would give attention only to rendering justice among men."[17]

This fundamental assumption that government may interfere and, in fact, must regulate the religious lives of the people was repudiated in the American constitutional experiment.[18] Standing

---

16. Calvin, *Institutes* IV.20.9. Wood makes the important point that "though Kuyper argued for an 'absolute' separation of church and state, he also argued that the magistrate had the responsibility to uphold both tables of the law" (*Going Dutch*, 111–12). This is reflected, for example, in his *Lectures on Calvinism*. He affirmed that magistrates have the duty "to restrain blasphemy, where it directly assumes the character of an affront to the Divine majesty." "The *duty* to exercise this right flows from the fact that God is the Supreme and Sovereign Ruler over every State and over every Nation." He went on to say, "What is then punished is not the religious offence, nor the impious sentiment, but the attack upon the foundation of public law, upon with both the State and its government are resting" (103).

17. Calvin, *Institutes* IV.20.9. The making of such a concession had a downside for Calvin. Calvin and his ministerial colleagues had to fight to maintain the autonomy of the church against the civil government of Geneva. Perhaps the classic example of this with respect to Calvin related to his desire for weekly communion. The government, however, only permitted the sacrament of the Lord's Supper four times a year—on Easter, Pentecost, the first Sunday in September, and Christmas. The government whose authority extended to the First Table of the Law dictated how the sacramental worship of God would be conducted. It did not matter that the theologians, namely Calvin, wanted a weekly communion.

18. Theologians in the ancient church were divided over the rise of caesaro-papism in the time of Constantine. Eusebius of Caesarea was a proponent of this model of church-state relations. In contrast to Eusebius, Ambrose forcefully stated that "Caesar's sway cannot extend over the temple of God." He put his position succinctly in this declaration: "The emperor is within the church, not above it" (*Sermon against Auxentius*, 75. Along these lines Chrysostom cited the example of Uzziah the ancient king of Judah who overreached the civil jurisdiction given to him by God. His attempt to take on the distinct calling of the priesthood resulted in God striking him with leprosy. He would thus "bear the trophy of his punishment like an inscription on a monument." This act of divine judgment "was not for his own sake, but for those who would follow him" (*The Fourth Homily on the Text: "I Saw the Lord*," 99). This was a warning

behind the First Amendment was Madison's argument that "religion" cannot be "subject to" the authority of a "legislative body." A legislative body has a "jurisdiction" that is "limited." Legislative bodies must not "overleap the great barrier which defends the rights of the people." It is the "unalienable right" of the people to worship God according to their "conviction and conscience."[19]

Madison's basic starting point with reference to his position regarding a limited jurisdiction was that "religion" was "not within the cognizance of civil government."[20] Thus, it was nothing but "an arrogant pretension" when government attempted to tear down the barrier of religious liberty. In fact, there was more involved than arrogance. "The rulers who are guilty of such an encroachment," Madison insisted, "are tyrants." Furthermore, "the people who submit to it . . . are slaves."[21]

Kuyper stood firmly within the Madisonian trajectory on the limited jurisdiction of civil government. With respect to government, Kuyper asked, "Must it . . . form an individual judgment, as to which of those many Churches is the true one? And must it maintain this one over against the others?" He answered his own questions by asserting that it is "the duty of the government to suspend its own judgment." Like Madison who affirmed that religion

---

according to Chrysostom to all politicians who would similarly intrude themselves into the affairs of the church. Chrysostom clearly drew the line between the distinct jurisdictions of church and state. He put it this way: "The king, then, is entrusted with the care of our bodies, the priest with our souls. The king may remit our financial debts, the priest remits our moral debts. The one uses coercion, the other persuasion. The one bears weapons that may be seen and felt, the other bears weapons of the spirit. The one goes to war against foreign hordes, whereas *my* war is against demons" (98). The quotations from Ambrose and Chrysostom are located in O'Donovan and O'Donovan, *From Irenaeus to Grotius*.

19. Madison, "Memorial and Remonstrance," 64.

20. Ibid., 66.

21. Ibid., 64. We should remember the European context of Madison's teaching. Pfeffer, *Church, State, and Freedom*, makes the point that the Spanish Inquisition established by Ferdinand and Isabella in 1480 continued to function until 1834. In fact, "as late at 1781 it caused heretics to be burned at the stake" (22). Indeed, "the Inquisition was still a reality in 1787 and the spirit of medieval intolerance was far from extinguished" (29).

is not within the cognizance of civil government, Kuyper reasoned that the government's suspension of judgment rests upon the fact that "the government lacks the data of judgment."[22] This is why the government must not "pose as a power above these different institutions" and then proceed "to render a decision between her and her sister-churches."[23]

What was Kuyper's assessment of a government that followed the Byzantine model of seeking "to extirpate every form of false religion" and of "bringing differences in religious matters under the criminal jurisdiction of the government"?[24] How did he respond to the medieval mindset of Thomas Aquinas—the same perspective that Calvin later embraced—that heretics "have deserved not only to be separated from the Church, but to be eliminated from the world by death"?[25] Kuyper believed that the "intervention of the government in the matter of religion"[26] should be seen as "the grasp of despotism."[27] Like Madison, he maintained that such

---

22. Kuyper, *Lectures on Calvinism*, 105.

23. Ibid., 106. In *De Gemeene Gratie*, 3.231–32, Kuyper said, "The relation of church and state undergoes no stronger change than through the splitting of the one visible church into many churches of different, even partly contradictory confession" (quoted in Wood, *Going Dutch*, 145). Wood notes that Kuyper was making the point that no government is "competent to decide among the myriad churches which was the one true church and which ones ought to be removed" (ibid.).

24. Kuyper, *Lectures on Calvinism*, 100.

25. *Summa Theologica* 2ae2ae, q. 11, art. 3, quoted from Aquinas, *Aquinas*, 79. Aquinas' basic assumption was that "it is a far graver matter to corrupt the faith which is the life of the soul than to falsify money which sustains the temporal life." Aquinas reasoned, "If it be just that forgers and other malefactors are put to death without mercy by the secular authority, with how much greater reason may heretics be not only excommunicated, but also put to death, when once they are convicted of heresy." The perspective of Robert Dabney was the total antithesis of the view of Aquinas. "Moral, merciful, peaceful men," he said, are "punished with the pains due to the most atrocious crimes, because they do not take certain arguments in a certain way" (*Systematic Theology*, 878). He further stated, "Religious sects are nearly harmless to the State, when they are no longer persecuted" (879).

26. Kuyper, *Lectures on Calvinism*, 99.

27. Ibid., 108.

tyranny brutalized the citizens and made them less than men: "In order that it may be able to rule *men*, the government must respect this deepest ethical power of our human existence." He concluded, "A nation, consisting of citizens whose consciences are bruised, is itself broken in its national strength."[28]

Church Disestablishment

We have reflected thus far upon the remarkable continuity of thought between Kuyper and the American tradition of religious liberty as it was articulated by perhaps its most eloquent spokesman, James Madison. At the same time, we have been reminded of the sharp contrast between Calvinian and neo-Calvinist thought on the same subject. We shall now turn our attention to the subject of church disestablishment. Once again, we find that Kuyper reflected the American constitutional commitment to disestablishment, a position that is not defended by Calvin.[29]

Madison first made a public statement in favor of disestablishment at the Virginia Convention in 1776. The Williamsburg convention not only declared independence from Great Britain, but it also produced a famous declaration of rights. Madison successfully, as we have seen, incorporated a freedom of religion clause in Article XVI of the Virginia Bill of Rights: "All men are equally entitled to the free exercise of religion, according to the dictates of conscience." Immediately following this clause, Madison wanted the introduction of the following clause regarding disestablishment: "And therefore that no man or class of men ought, on account of

---

28. Ibid.
29. Handy, "The Magna Charta," 303, reminds us of how significant the constitutional provision for disestablishment actually was: "When we remember that in 1750 there were church establishments of one kind or another in nine of the 13 colonies, and recall how deeply imbedded in the western tradition the ideal of establishment was, the constitutional events that set the new nation on the path of religious freedom show their revolutionary significance."

religion to be invested with peculiar emoluments or privileges."[30] Madison's attempt to include legal disestablishment failed.[31]

Disestablishment would have to wait until 1786 when Jefferson's Statute for Religious Freedom was passed by the Virginia legislature. In 1784, however, it was by no means certain that church disestablishment would triumph in Virginia. In that year Patrick Henry and others introduced a bill in which a general assessment would be levied to support all Christian ministers of whatever denomination they happened to belong.[32] This would, in effect, amount to a "multiple establishment."[33] Henry's bill was eventually defeated, but it was the springboard for the production of Madison's "Memorial and Remonstrance" of 1785. In this famous statement of protest, he laid out his reasons for opposing the bill in question and produced a political manifesto for the ages, "an argument in defense of freedom for the human mind worthy of Milton, Jefferson, or Mill."[34]

Before we examine Madison's major arguments against church establishment, we should point out that Madison's political philosophy on this issue was no doubt shaped by his experience. Madison's distaste for a state-supported church arose from his experience in Virginia where the government supported the wayward Anglican ministry, while at the same time imprisoned zealous and sincere Baptist preachers—thus denying to them the freedom to practice their religion.[35] At the same time, his desire for disestablishment and his love of religious liberty were nurtured while he studied at the College of New Jersey in Princeton. He had

30. Ketcham, *James Madison*, 72.

31. Ketcham states, "Since the clause, if adopted, would have wiped out the establishment of the Anglican Church, it alarmed enough men to cause its defeat" (ibid., 72).

32. Durham and Sewell, "Virginia Founders," 71, affirm that the bill "allowed individuals to specify the church to which their tax moneys would go." Furthermore, people who did not wish to support a church "would be able to earmark their funds for their local schools."

33. Handy, "The Magna Charta," 308.

34. Ketcham, *James Madison*, 163.

35. Loconte, "Faith and the Founding," 699.

seen the difference between Presbyterian pastors in New Jersey and Anglican priests in Virginia. On the basis of his own experience, he came to the fundamental conviction that disestablishment and freedom resulted in greater sincerity in the practice of religion.[36]

Madison presented two broad arguments in his treatise against church establishment. In the first place, he maintained that the church did not need to be supported by the taxes of the people and that the church actually prospered more without taxation. "The establishment proposed by the Bill is not requisite for the support of the Christian Religion," he stated.[37] Referring to the pre-Constantinian period, he declared, "This Religion both existed and flourished, not only without the support of human laws, but in spite of every opposition from them." The period of Christianity's "greatest luster" was in "the ages prior to its incorporation with civil policy."[38] Interestingly enough, we find that Kuyper spoke in virtually identical terms. He asserted "that Churches flourish most richly when the government allows them to live from their own strength on the voluntary principle."[39]

The second major argument that Madison proposed related to the deleterious effects of church establishment. It was not beneficial for Christians: "It is moreover to weaken in those who profess this Religion, a pious confidence in its innate excellence, and the patronage of its author." In addition, it was not beneficial for non-Christians. It helped "to foster in those who still reject it, a suspicion that its friends are too conscious of its fallacies to trust it to its own merits." Establishment, he further argued, had a bad impact upon ministers, bringing "pride and indolence in the clergy." It inevitably led to "bigotry and persecution."[40]

In terms of its long-range implications, Madison worried about "the consequence" that could flow out of "the principle." The demand upon the citizen to support a particular religion with

---

36. Wills, *James Madison*, 18.
37. Madison, "Memorial and Remonstrance," 65.
38. Ibid.
39. Kuyper, *Lectures on Calvinism*, 106.
40. Madison, "Memorial and Remonstrance," 65.

his money would eventually lead to the demand of total religious conformity: "The same authority which can force a citizen to contribute three pence only of his property for the support of any one establishment, may force him to conform to any other establishment in all cases whatsoever."[41] In the view of Madison, religious establishment puts certain citizens on a lower level than others: "It degrades from the equal rank of citizens all those whose opinions in religion do not bend to those of the legislative authority." Eventually, over time, it would lead to something like the Inquisition: "Distant as it may be, in its present form, from the Inquisition, it differs from it only in degree." He elaborated, "The one is the first step, the other the last, in the career of intolerance."[42]

As Kuyper commented upon the American constitutional rejection of a Constantinian state-church alliance, he made a statement worthy of Madison: "The separation of church and state . . . proceeds . . . from . . . the realization that the well-being of the church and the progress of Christianity demand it."[43]

Conclusion

It is quite remarkable when the head of a political party in another country appeals to the First Amendment of the American Constitution in support of his own program. This is precisely what Abraham Kuyper did as the leader of the Antirevolutionary Party. He wanted to demonstrate to the Dutch people that church disestablishment and full religious liberty along with vital Christianity are much more than an idealistic dream.[44] Such a society,

---

41. Ibid., 64.

42. Ibid., 66. In his Princeton Theological Seminary *Lectures on Calvinism*, Kuyper spoke about the fact that "the deeply rooted repugnance against the Inquisition, which for three long centuries would not be assuaged, grew up from the conviction that its practices violated and assaulted human life" (107–8).

43. Kuyper, "Calvinism," 290–91.

44. Kuyper advocated the doctrine of a free church, a church that was "absolutely separated from the state." "In practical terms, separation of church and state meant giving churches control over their own property," and "it meant

he contended, was a reality in nineteenth-century America.[45] In his enthusiasm for both Calvin and the American experiment in church-state relations, he drew the conclusion that the seeds of Calvinian doctrine germinated and came to full growth in his own neo-Calvinist political philosophy. This chapter demonstrates that the perspective of Kuyper on church and state is, in reality, rooted in the American tradition.

We shall see in the next two chapters that his perspective on the church and social reformation stands in continuity with the Calvinist tradition. More specifically, we shall consider the contemporary problem in the United States of judicial tyranny and the subject of resistance and reform that is initiated by the church.

---

that the state should stop subsidizing the salaries of ministers" (Wood, *Going Dutch*, 70).

45. It is true that disestablishment occurred in the Netherlands in 1848. "Implementing this new arrangement, however, was not straightforward or immediate. As a pastor at Utrecht, Kuyper was paid out of state coffers" (Wood, *Going Dutch*, 61). In fact, the churches in the Netherlands continued to be subsidized by the state until the 1980s, when it was completely abolished (ibid., 143).

6

Tyranny

APART FROM GRACE EVERY culture tends to decline and degenerate. This indeed is the great lesson of ancient history. Kuyper remarked, "The ancient history of all people replays a shameful spectacle." "The freedom of the spheres dies out and State power—become Caesarism—triumphs." "As antiquity drew toward its close there was no freedom left, no nations, no spheres."[1] From a Calvinistic perspective human society is "like a carcass slowly but surely deteriorating, disintegrating, and rotting to putrefaction."[2] It desperately needs a powerful influence to stay the corruption.

Social Transformation

Calvinists have noted that the church in its long history has not only blunted the forces of evil, but it has also brought blessing, transformation, and reformation to the world.[3] Calvin looked for

---

1. Kuyper, "Sphere Sovereignty," 469.
2. Lawlor, *The Beatitudes*, 108.
3. Lutheran theology has tended to emphasize more the idea that the church acts as a retardant to prevent the downward spiral of moral degeneration in a society. Cf., Smith, *The Universe*, 234; Troeltsch, *The Social Teaching*, 2:563. Clarke, *Our Southern Zion*, 5, makes the point that the Reformed tradition has had a "radical impulse"—referring to the fact that it so often "seeks the transformation of society" and "dreams of holy commonwealths and a new Zion."

the present permeation of all life by the gospel.[4] He was determined to engage with the world, seeking to claim the world for its creator. More specifically, he valued economics. He endorsed cities with all of their activities along with business and trade. The concern of Calvin was not to escape from the world, but rather to tether it to the Word of God.[5]

Calvinists have envisioned societies that are both virtuous and free.[6] There is the recognition that such a social order is a singular favor from the Heavenly Father, "a *gift* from God."[7] As Kuyper contemplated the rise of freedom among the Dutch people, he affirmed, "That freedom came from above. The God who is Love sent it to us."[8]

This societal hope may be expressed in the language of Scripture. "Let justice run down like water, and righteousness like a mighty stream" (Amos 5:24). It may be affirmed in the testimony of the church father Justin Martyr who wrote about the societal impact of the gospel: "We who were filled with war, and mutual slaughter, and every wickedness, have each through the whole earth changed our warlike weapons—our swords into ploughshares, and our spears into implements of tillage—and we cultivate piety, righteousness, philanthropy, faith, and hope."[9] It may be maintained in the words of Kuyper who stated that "the primordial and inalienable right of all men" is "liberty of conscience" for "each and every citizen," which necessarily includes "*liberty of speech*" and "*liberty of worship.*"[10]

The good and the free society are at the heart of what Calvinists have longed for as a result of the transformative power of the gospel.[11] There is also no question that we Americans have

---

4. Niebuhr, *Christ and Culture*, 217.
5. Graham, *The Constructive Revolutionary*, 198.
6. Thornwell, "Sermon on National Sins," 521.
7. Abraham Kuyper, "Freedom," 319.
8. Ibid.
9. Martyr, *Dialogue with Trypho*, 254.
10. Kuyper, *Lectures on Calvinism*, 108; italics original.
11. Spykman, "The Principled Pluralist," 78, 80–81.

enjoyed significant elements of this kind of society. As Kuyper contemplated the United States from a European perspective, he concluded that "modern liberties flourish in America." He delineated what he meant in terms of these specifics:

"There is complete freedom of conscience, freedom to start an enterprise and to engage in commerce, freedom for citizens to participate in public affairs." He added, "There is a duly responsible government, a small army, low taxation, freedom of organization, a free press, freedom of worship, and freedom of opinion.[12]

Abusive Government

Calvin himself believed that those who are "permitted to enjoy" a society "where freedom is regulated with becoming moderation" are to be reckoned the "most happy."[13] All threats therefore to the realization of such a social vision are matters of great alarm.[14] No doubt tyranny ever remains the preeminent threat to the shining city on a hill. Kuyper declared that it is against "State-omnipotence" and "the pride of absolutism" that "Calvinism protests," and it further maintains that "the struggle for liberty is not only

---

12. Kuyper, "Calvinism," 286.

13. Calvin, *Institutes* IV.20.8.

14. The great threats to freedom in the twentieth century were totalitarian movements, which despised liberal societies. As Berman puts it, *Terror and Liberalism*, 37–38, a liberal society is one in which there is "freedom of thought and freedom of religion." There are "free elections, political parties, opposition newspapers," "privacy," and "tolerance" (162). Liberal societies have aroused "feelings of violent revulsion" (xiii). Totalitarian movements over the course of the last century maintained that our civilization "ought to be destroyed as quickly and violently as possible" (42). In place of freedom, they advocated "the ideal of submission." There was to be "submission to" the "total state, the total doctrine, the total movement." Totalitarian movements did not like the idea that individuals may freely pursue happiness as they see fit. In their view, everyone must think alike and pursue the exact same things. "It was the ideal of the one, instead of the many" (46). The state would determine ultimate meaning for the masses, who would dare not question what is imposed upon them.

declared permissible, but is made a duty for each individual in his own sphere."[15]

At times, the fact of tyranny is more blatant. It entails, as Calvin noted, the "slaughtering" of "the innocent."[16] Such tyrants are manifest to all: they are beasts who "violently fall upon and assault the lowly common folk."[17]

From another viewpoint, tyranny can be explained in terms of its relationship to law. Tyranny is "authority setting itself against the laws."[18] It "strives with might and maim to subvert the constitution."[19] One type of tyranny occurs when the magistrate "violates, changes, or overthrows the fundamental laws of the realm."[20] Such tyranny, as Calvin noted, is often found in "the courts of justice." It may involve judges who have "spared murderers," or the same judges may have "deprived miserable men of their right."[21] "Tyrants" are those who "confound good and evil, right and wrong."[22]

Violence against "the lowly common folk" and subversion of the laws are unmistakable traits of tyrannical government. The absence of freedom is another dominant characteristic. The tyrant sees to it, observed Calvin, that "all liberty shall be taken away." Specifically, "tyrannical violence" sees to it that "no freedom of speech" is "allowed." "Tyrants would impose silence on all teachers" who would dare to bring a word of reproof against them— "now throwing them into prisons, then banishing them."[23]

There are, however, somewhat more subtle forms of tyranny. The point has been made that tyrants are more than ready to say, "We are the law." Their fundamental assumption is that "they at

---

15. Kuyper, *Lectures on Calvinism*, 98–99.
16. Calvin, *Institutes* IV.20.24.
17. Ibid., IV.20.31.
18. Beza, *Concerning the Rights of Rulers*, 48.
19. Ibid., 80.
20. Althusius, *Politica*, 192.
21. Calvin, *Commentaries on the Prophet Amos*, 269–70.
22. Calvin, *Commentary on the Book of Psalms*, 336.
23. Calvin, *Commentaries on the Prophet Amos*, 271–72.

their pleasure may command what they list, and that all men by and by must take it for law." This kind of governance "is extreme tyranny."[24] The ruler that believes that he is the source of the law is a tyrant, because "power and authority" ought rather to be "subjects unto laws."[25] God in fact "has ordered" the magistrates "to be conservators" of the law.[26] The laws that are so maintained come from the people. "The people is the parent, or at least the author of the law, and has the power of its enactment or repeal at pleasure."[27] "The people" must "be the fountain of laws."[28]

As we have seen, the political and social conception of Calvinistic thought has focused upon the vision for a society that is known for its commitment to the rule of law, freedom, and virtue. Any threat to the maintenance of such a social order has been regarded with alarm. Tyranny in particular has been considered to be a major danger to the shining city on a hill. Lawless governmental acts, the trampling down of religious liberty, and the sanctioning of the slaughter of the innocent are some of the more blatant characteristics of tyrannical government.

Judicial Tyranny

It should be obvious to students of American law and politics that freedom and virtue in the contemporary American scene have been diminished. The significant erosion of liberty and social righteousness in modern America has been largely instigated by activist courts. It is quite clear from the perspective of Calvinian political thought that tyrants sit on the bench in many of our federal courts. A number of constitutional scholars have made this point. Lino Graglia refers to "the justices of the Supreme Court" as a powerful nine-person elite, in other words, a "tyranny by a

---

24. Bullinger, *The Decades of Henry Bullinger*, 339.
25. Ibid.
26. Buchanan, *The Rights of the Crown*, 269.
27. Ibid., 276.
28. Rutherford, *The Law and the Prince*, 114.

minority."²⁹ John Whitehead speaks of the federal judiciary as "an oligarchy that answers to no one." He expresses his fear that "power in government has indeed passed to those who act tyrannically."³⁰ Robert Bork asserts that "the democratic nation is helpless before an antidemocratic, indeed a despotic judiciary."³¹

We are not referring here to judges who take the view of former United States Supreme Court Chief Justice William H. Rehnquist who properly stated, "Justices of the Supreme Court have a great deal of authority, but it is not an authority to weave into the Constitution their own ideas of what is good and what is bad."³² Nor are we speaking about jurists like former Alabama Chief Justice Roy Moore who maintains that "judges must always rule according to law," recognizing that they are not super-legislators with the power to make law at the stroke of a pen."³³ We are discussing judges who embrace the judicial philosophy that "the Constitution is what the judges say it is."³⁴ We are drawing

---

29. Graglia, "Constitutional Law," 4–5. The same point has been made by Levin in his best-selling *Men in Black*, 10. Levin laments that "America has turned from the most representative form of government to a de facto judicial tyranny."

30. Whitehead, *The Second American Revolution*, 71–72.

31. Bork, *Slouching Towards Gomorrah*, 119. Cf., Bork, *The Tempting of America*, 140.

32. Rehnquist, *The Supreme Court*, 314. Rehnquist makes the candid admission, "Every judge who has sat on a case involving a constitutional claim must have surely experienced the feeling that the particular law being challenged was either unjust, or silly, or vindictive. It is unfortunately all too easy to translate these visceral reactions into a determination to find some way to hold the law unconstitutional" (ibid.).

33. Moore, *So Help Me God*, 165.

34. Quoted in Whitehead, *The Second American Revolution*, 20. This quip was once made by the Supreme Court Chief Justice Charles Evans Hughes. The sentiments of Chief Justice Hughes were much different than those of Chief Justice John Marshall. In *Marbury v. Madison*, 5 U. S. 179–180, Marshall wrote that "it is apparent, that the framers of the constitution contemplated that instrument as a rule for the government of courts" (quoted in Moore, *So Help Me God*, 215).

attention here to justices who say, "You do what you think is right and let the law catch up."[35]

Absolutism and tyranny are nothing new. Today, proponents of an imperial judiciary remain untroubled by absolutist judges who regard themselves as an intellectual elite standing above the law,[36] constructing novel interpretations that continually rewrite Constitution so that it becomes an increasingly radical document.[37]

The Court essentially twists the Constitution into a code of philosophical principles that provide protection for freedom regarded as license. An example of this is seen in *Lawrence v. Texas* (2003), which overturned the laws of Texas that prohibited homosexual sodomy.[38] Writing for the majority, Justice Anthony Kennedy affirmed that the constitutional commitment to liberty "includes freedom of thought, belief, expression and certain

---

35. Rhode, "A Tribute," 1259. This statement from Justice Marshall illustrates the very thing George Washington warned against in his "Farewell Address," 221, in which he stated, "The spirit of encroachment tends to consolidate the powers of all the departments in one, and thus to create, whatever the form of government, a real despotism."

36. Harvard professor Abraham Chayes likes the idea of government by judiciary. In his piece "The Role of the Judge," 1307–8, Chayes argues that lawyers are able to engage in a "reflective and dispassionate analysis" of problems that come before them. A judge is able, he maintains, to be insulated against "narrow political pressures."

37. In *The Tempting of America*, Bork contends that for many judges "the Constitution and statutes" are "malleable texts that judges may rewrite to see that particular groups or political causes may win" (2). He states, "Today's constitutional cognoscenti ... would have judges remake the historic Constitution." The result is that a "new constitutional law is much more egalitarian and socially permissive than either the actual Constitution or the legislative opinion of the American public" (6). Later, Bork uses the language of "the Supreme Court's rewriting of the Constitution" (145).

38. I am not here addressing the subject as to whether or not the state of Texas ought to have laws prohibiting sodomy. The issue at hand is the very narrow one as to whether or not the United States Constitution grants such a right to American citizens. It is unacceptable for the Supreme Court to manipulate the Constitution into whatever kind of document they desire it to be and thereby to read their own values into it.

intimate conduct."[39] According to the majority, the Constitution does in fact protect the freedom and the right of sodomy. The Constitution, however, was not the only authority that Kennedy cited. He also appealed to the European Convention on Human Rights and the decisions of the European Court of Human Rights. Kennedy wrote concerning *Lawrence v. Texas*, "The right the petitioners seek in this case has been accepted as an integral part of freedom in many other countries."[40]

It is ironic that the very court that implements the principle of freedom without restriction or limitation has so often ruled against the free expression of religion within the public square. We have come a long way since Kuyper published his *Het Calvinisme, oorsprong en waarborg onzer constitutioneele vrijheden* in 1874. Speaking about America, Kuyper observed that the principle of separation of church and state "does not prevent sessions of Congress, political conventions and meetings from being opened with prayer." He then stated, "The public school in America is a school with the Bible" and "in America a public school without the Bible would be simply unthinkable."[41]

In recent years, however, the Supreme Court has stood in opposition to the freedom of religion clause of the First Amendment as it has been historically understood. It has likewise contradicted the stance of the Declaration of Independence, the foundational constituting law of the United States. While the Declaration publicly expresses faith in the "firm reliance on the protection of Divine Providence," the Supreme Court promotes an agenda of removing God from public life, keeping "a wall of separation between church and state," a wall that "must be kept high and impregnable."[42]

39. Quoted in McDowell, "The Perverse Paradox of Privacy," 58.
40. Quoted in Levin, *Men in Black*, 20.
41. Kuyper, "Calvinism," 291.
42. *Everson v. Board of Ed. of Ewing*, 330 U. S. 1, 3 (1947). Quoted in Levin, *Men in Black*, 42. In the Everson ruling, Hugo Black appealed to Thomas Jefferson's 1802 letter to the Danbury Baptist Association. Justice Black lifted the expression "a wall of separation between church and state" from the letter. On the basis of this phrase, he contended, "Neither a state nor the Federal Government can, openly or secretly, participate in the affairs of any religious

The problematic nature of such constitutional reasoning is patent. Judge Roy Moore asks, "How could the Declaration of Independence, an 'organic' law of our nation according to the present United States Code Annotated—a compilation of the laws of the United States—declare God to be the author of our rights and Creator of all mankind, while the acknowledgment of God is considered a violation of the First Amendment, according to judges and lawyers?"[43]

When one considers some of the major rulings of the Supreme Court over the last two generations—*Engel v. Vitale* (1962) that struck down state-sponsored, but voluntary, student prayer;[44] *Abington v. Schempp* (1963) that overthrew state-sponsored, but voluntary, Bible reading and reciting of the Lord's Prayer; and *Stone v. Graham* (1980) that disallowed the display of the Ten Commandments in public schools of Kentucky, even though paid for by private donations—it becomes quite clear that Chief Justice William Rehnquist did not exaggerate when he declared that the Supreme Court "bristles with hostility to all things religious in public life."[45]

Kuyper's reflections upon the liberal agenda apply to our current situation in the United States: "The liberal seeks to restrict

---

organizations or groups and *vice versa.*" Black thus left the impression that Jefferson wanted to keep religion completely out of public life. The Jefferson letter, however, went on to state, "I reciprocate your kind prayers for the protection and blessing of the common Father and Creator of man" (quoted in Witte, *Religion*, 56). Contextually, the Danbury letter indicates that when Jefferson referred to "a wall of separation between church and state" he meant that the church and liberty of conscience were protected by the First Amendment from the intrusions of the state (ibid., 55–56).

43. Moore, *So Help Me God*, 49.

44. In *Engel v. Vitale*, Justice Hugo Black asserted that the following prayer was unconstitutional: "Almighty God, we acknowledge our dependence upon Thee and we beg Thy blessings upon us, our parents, our teachers, and our Country." See Moore, *So Help Me God*, 49.

45. Quoted in Eastland, "A Court Tilting," 97. Such efforts to "privatize theistic religion" is tied in with the fact that "core Enlightenment beliefs" in the twentieth century "came to more direct legal expression" (Witte, "God's Joust," 306).

and enclose the life of faith within the most strictly confined and private limits while we seek exactly the opposite, the expansion of faith's power and influence as far as possible."[46]

Constitutional Subversion

Tyranny exists in the United States from the standpoint of Calvinian doctrine on this subject. The imperial judiciary is the fountainhead of constitutional subversion. Indeed, much of contemporary constitutional law has very little to do with the Constitution. "Nearly all the Supreme Court's rulings of constitutionality have little or no basis in, and are sometimes in direct violation of, the Constitution."[47] What then is the outcome when judges stray from their obligation to apply the Constitution and the law to the cases that come before them? They undermine the Constitution. Such judges "destroy the very rule of law they claim to enforce."[48]

The result of setting aside the supreme law of the land—particularly in *Roe v. Wade*, a decision without constitutional basis—has been the slaughter of the innocent, the unborn in their mothers' wombs.[49] This indeed, as Ronald Reagan put it in his 1986 State of the Union address, is the great "wound in our national conscience."[50] In violation of the Constitution, such persons—"at least 35 million over the first twenty-five years after

---

46. John Bolt provides the translation of this passage from *Ons Program* in "Abraham Kuyper and the Search," 154.
47. Graglia, "Constitutional Law," 2.
48. Levin, *Men in Black*, 18.
49. In his book *Abortion and the Conscience of the Nation*, Ronald Reagan drew attention to this most obvious fact: "Make no mistake, abortion-on-demand is not a right granted by the Constitution. No serious scholar, including one disposed to agree with the Court's result, has argued that the framers of the Constitution intended to create such a right. Shortly after the *Roe v. Wade* decision, Professor John Hart Ely, now Dean of Stanford Law School, wrote that the opinion 'is not constitutional law and give almost no sense of trying to be.'" Reagan went on to say that the decision was an "act of raw judicial power" (16).
50. Quoted in Kengor, *God and Ronald Reagan*, 178.

Roe"[51]—have been deprived of life without due process of law (Fifth Amendment). In violation of the Declaration of Independence, the foundational constituting law of the American Republic, the Supreme Court has denied the inalienable right of life given by the Creator.[52]

Reflecting the long history of Christian reflection on theological ethics, Calvin affirmed that "the *foetus*, though enclosed in the womb of its mother, is already a human being." He added, "If it seems more horrible to kill a man in his own house than in a field, because a man's house is his place of most secure refuge, it ought surely to be deemed more atrocious to destroy a *foetus* in the womb before it has come to light."[53] According to the Supreme Court, however, many state legislative efforts to protect that life in the womb are unconstitutional. Thus, the Constitution in the hands of an activist Supreme Court can hardly be viewed as "the gift of God, the mold of equity, a standard of justice, a likeness of the Divine Will" and "the guardian of well-being."[54]

Graglia wonders why these judicial usurpations of legislative power are allowed to continue.[55] He suggests that part of the reason has to do with the fact that Americans seem to be awed by the majesty and dignity of the judicial office.

There is no question, as Calvin put it, that "we ought to show respect to judges . . . as the Lord has honoured them with dignified

---

51. Schweikert and Allen, *A Patriot's History*, 734.

52. Berns, *Taking the Constitution Seriously*, 23, draws attention to the fact that the Declaration of Independence is listed in a number of legal documents—including *The Public Statutes at Large of the United States of America* (1854), the *Revised Statutes of the United States* (1878), and *The Federal and State Constitutions, Colonial Charters, and Other Organic Laws of the United States* (1877). Berns makes the point that the Declaration is classified as an organic law in the *United States Code*. "An organic law is an organizing or constituting law." It was through the instrument of the Declaration of Independence that men such as Washington, Jefferson, Franklin, and others joined to form a new society, which would become the American Republic (25).

53. Calvin, *Commentaries on the Last Four Books of Moses*, 41–42.

54. John of Salisbury, *Policraticus* VIII.17.

55. Graglia, "Constitutional Law," 11.

titles, calling them his vicegerents and also gods."⁵⁶ Respect, however, is not to overleap its boundaries. What Kuyper stated concerning kings certainly applies to all judges: "If God alone is sovereign, and if each of us, including the king, is a creature that depends on Him, then all adoration of kings as individuals, any attempt to see a king as a higher form of being, is base robbery of the glory of his name."⁵⁷

Judges alone, Graglia reminds us, "dress in robes and issue decrees from structures resembling temples." He goes on to say that "the public understandably wants to believe" that judges are "servants of the law, protectors from powerful and untrustworthy bureaucrats and other governmental officials."⁵⁸

The aura of the courtroom creates the impression in the minds of many that the judges who preside are somehow unlike the politicians who have a public policy agenda.⁵⁹ The facts are much different than the perception. Graglia states concerning Supreme Court justices, "Their only professional qualification is that they must be lawyers, professionally skilled in the manipulation of language to achieve a predetermined result. Nothing in the study or practice of law is calculated to inculcate exceptional candor, ethical refinement, or habits of intellectual integrity." The hard truth is that "the study or practice of law is more likely to inculcate the ability to blur the distinction between truth and falsehood."⁶⁰

This severe assessment of the state of contemporary legal education and practice should come as no surprise to students of sixteenth-century Reformed political theory. Bullinger affirmed that "the vices that are in judges be many, and the diseases of their minds are sundry."⁶¹ Commenting upon the situation in Eng-

---

56. Calvin, *Commentaries on the Prophet Micah*, 238.

57. Kuyper, "Calvinism," 308.

58. Graglia, "Constitutional Law," 11–12.

59. When Kuyper visited Washington, DC in the fall of 1898, he met with President William McKinley, and also "attended a session of the Supreme Court" (Kuyper, *Kuyper in America*, 71).

60. Ibid., 40.

61. Bullinger, *The Decades of Henry Bullinger*, 348.

land, Bucer referred to the "many dreadful complaints" that were "publicly circulated." He specified that "trials throughout the realm take place under men" who were "openly avaricious and ready to take bribes and given to other vices so that the judgments rendered by them" were "in many ways vicious and corrupt."[62]

Calvin who was trained in the law schools of Orléans and Bourges had a similar perspective concerning the judges of his time. He wrote about "the monstrous stupidity of judges, who can remain indifferent and unmoved in horrible confusion of civil society."[63] He referred to an "evil" that "commonly prevails." "At this day," he said, "the cruelty of many judges appears especially in this—that they hunt for crimes for the sake of gain." He was here referring to judges who looked for bribes and who were more than willing to spare murderers and robbers, "not indeed without rewards."[64]

Kuyper's words regarding monarchs certainly apply to judges: "Kings are sinners too. Being tempted more severely they will succumb even sooner than their subjects."

There may, however, be another reason why judicial usurpations of power are allowed to continue. While many Americans are probably oblivious to the erosion of their freedom at the hands of judicial despots, it may well be the case that others do not even care. Gresham Machen already made this observation early in the twentieth century about government in general: "No interference is resented today, no menace to family life, no government monopoly, if only it be thought to confer physical benefits."[65] To what did Machen attribute the widespread lack of resentment at governmental interference? Why was the "healthy hatred of being governed, formerly so strong in the American people," ever so "gradually being lost"?[66] The fundamental problem, argued Machen, was spiritual and moral.[67] The rise of tyranny and the erosion

62. Bucer, *On the Kingdom of Christ*, 374.
63. Calvin, *Commentary on the Book of Psalms*, 334.
64. Calvin, *Commentaries on the Prophet Amos*, 269.
65. Machen, *Education, Christianity, and the State*, 138.
66. Ibid.
67. Later in the century, Ronald Reagan would express his own sense that

of freedom ultimately "had its roots in a fundamental deterioration of the American people." Specifically, "the people has come to value principle less and creature comfort more; increasingly it has come to prefer prosperity to freedom."[68]

Kuyper had similar concerns about the Netherlands in the nineteenth century. He affirmed that "the indifference of the people" resulted in "freedom" being "in danger." He sensed that many of the Dutch had become "totally blasé" and were "no longer enthused for an idea, a right, a particular freedom."[69]

What shall we do in times such as these?

We ought to remember that we have a moral obligation. Kuyper reminded his generation: "The struggle for liberty is not only declared permissible, but is made a duty for each individual in his own sphere."[70] We turn our attention to the nature of this struggle in the next chapter—reflecting upon the responsibility of the church, the task of the Christian citizen, and the duty of the state on the issue of resisting and reforming the American judiciary.

America needed revival. Note his letter addressed to Greg Brezina of Fayetteville, Georgia, dated October 25, 1982, published in *Reagan: A Life in Letters*, 654.

68. Machen, *Education, Christianity, and the* State, 67.

69. Kuyper, "Calvinism," 282–83.

70. Kuyper, *Lectures on Calvinism*, 98–99.

7

Resistance and Reform

RESISTANCE TO TYRANNY, AND more than that, the reform of the judiciary begins in the church with the faithful preaching of the whole counsel of God, which would necessarily include expounding upon the doctrine of the state as it surfaces in various passages in the biblical text in a ministry committed to consecutive expository preaching. Such teaching would include positive instruction on the role of a judge as it is set forth in Scripture. This teaching would encourage Christians to be active citizens in the political process.[1] The voting of such biblically instructed citizens would entail voting for presidents who are committed to the appointing of originalists to the federal courts. It would also mean that representatives and senators would be elected who understand that they have an important role in providing resistance to judicial tyranny.

Let us now examine these matters in their proper order. We begin with the ministry of the church as an institution.[2]

---

1. Wood, *Going Dutch*, 13, draws attention to the Reveil party in the Netherlands, which resulted from a spiritual revival that swept through the country in the early nineteenth century. The movement included Guillaume Groen van Prinsterer, jurist, historian, and secretary of the king's cabinet. Reveil spirituality focused upon inward piety. In the view of Kuyper, they seemed to have a phobia of becoming active in the political arena. "Not only did they fail to carry their Calvinist principles into politics; they also seemed to be afraid of politics altogether, partly due to the residual influence of the pietistic Reveil movement that had focused religion inward" (161).

2. Kuyper insisted that the church is both organism and institution. In "Common Grace," 187–88, he wrote, "That church is an *organism* insofar as

The Proclamation of the Church

How shall the church respond to the rise of tyranny within a nation? The historic Calvinist view is that the proclamation of the church with respect to tyranny should be twofold.[3] On the one hand, it should offer an annihilating critique of sin in the state; while on the other hand, it should instruct and exhort the state in the way of righteousness.[4] As Kuyper put it, the church as an institution "works formatively upon the individual, structurally upon the family, *directively upon society*."[5]

---

we view it in its hidden unity as the mystical body of Christ existing partly in heaven, partly on earth, and partly unborn, having penetrated all peoples and nations, possessing Christ as its natural and glorious head, and living by the Holy Spirit who as a life-engendering and life-maintaining force animates both head and members. Viewed as *institute*, on the other hand, the church is an *apparatus*, a local and temporally constructed *institution* grounded in human choices, decisions, and acts of the will, consisting of members, offices, and useful supplies. As such it is a phenomenon in the external, visible, and perceptible world, something you can see with your eyes, hear with your ears, and touch with your hands but having real substance only insofar as the mystical body of Christ lies behind it and manifests itself through it, however imperfectly. When that ceases to be the case, the institute is no longer a church except in appearance, a false church."

3. In Kuyper's perspective, a discussion of the proclamation of the church immediately relates to the church as an institution. In *Rooted and Grounded*, 15, he affirmed, "For neither the proclamation of that Word nor the administration of that sacrament is an organic operation. They presuppose human consciousness; they need human organization; they require a human act. They do not operate automatically, but through man as the instrument of the Lord. Their figurative representation is not that of something growing from a root, but of something being constructed on a foundation."

4. Kuyper, *Christianity*, 81. Cf., Berkhof, *The Church and Social Problems*, 18; Chadwick, *The Reformation*, 85–86. Thornwell, "Address to All Churches of Christ," 450, stated, "When the state makes wicked laws, contradicting the eternal principles of rectitude, the Church is at liberty to testify against them." The teaching of Thornwell though included more than the negative. He gave positive instruction on what the state is to do. In the most general sense, government is to have a beneficial purpose for the people. It is to be an "instrument of good." More specifically, the state exists for the realization of "social" order, and the concept of order is intimately related to the realization of justice (449).

5. Kuyper, *Rooted and Grounded*, 17; emphasis added. Wood comments

Calvin took the same view, exemplifying an awareness of the twofold task of the church with respect to the state in his discussion of the judiciary in his biblical commentaries. He recognized that "those who occupy the seats of judgment wish to be exempt from all reproofs . . . inasmuch as they think not that they belong to the common class of men, and imagine themselves exempt from all reprehension." In fact, "they complain and cry out, whenever teachers and God's servants dare to denude their wicked conduct." Nevertheless, the "vices" in judges "require strong remedies," namely, the medicine of strong reproofs. Calvin also understood that judges who have "perverted justice and right" are also those who reject "admonitions," and have "even hated them." But they nevertheless needed to be warned that "they themselves also must one day appear at the judgment-seat of heaven to render up an account."[6] With respect to judges, preachers "ought . . . to correct whatever is deserving of reproof, and not to spare even the chief men themselves."[7] Furthermore, the servants of God must be remembered as those who have "reminded them of their duty."[8]

Kuyper stood with Calvin on this issue, directly referring to Christianity and its influence upon law and justice. He said, "Though the lamp of the Christian religion only burns within that institute's walls, its light shines out through its windows to areas far beyond, illumining all the sectors and associations that appear across the wide range of human life and activity." He insisted, "*Justice, law*, the home and family, business, vocation, public opinion and literature, art and science, and so much more *are* all *illumined by that light*, and that illumination will be stronger and more penetrating as the lamp of the gospel is allowed to shine more brightly and clearly in the church institute.[9]

---

regarding Kuyper, "Although he believed in the separation of church and state, the church could not retreat or refrain from its social responsibility" (*Going Dutch*, 50). Cf., Skillen, "Politics, Pluralism," 198.

6. Calvin, *Commentary on the Book of Psalms*, 334–35.
7. Calvin, *Commentaries on the Prophet Micah*, 238.
8. Calvin, *Commentaries on the Prophet Amos*, 265.
9. Kuyper, "Common Grace," 194; emphasis added. Kuyper stated, "A

In a highly nuanced study on church and state, the Calvinist exegete John Murray reminded us that the church is not to engage in politics.[10] He qualified this position with the affirmation that church members must do so, "but only in their capacity as citizens of the state, not as members of the church."[11] He also warned, "The representatives of the church in the performance of their official ministrations must beware of turning the pulpit into a forum for the discussion of political questions, especially a forum for political partisanship."[12] Against the background of these words of caution, Murray directed the attention of the church to its twofold task of rebuking sin and instructing in the way of righteousness.[13]

Murray made the point that the call to proclaim the whole counsel of God is committed to the church, which means "the counsel of God as it bears upon the responsibility of all persons and institutions." This means that the church has a message of criticism directed against tyranny, which has lodged itself within the institution of the state. Specifically, if a political leader goes

---

sanctifying and purifying influence must proceed from the church of the Lord to impact the whole society amid which it operates." "It must purify and ennoble the ideas in general circulation, elevate public opinion, introduce more solid principles, and so raise the view of life prevailing in state, society, and the family" (ibid., 195).

10. Indeed, the Reformed insist that the church is neither a political party, nor the tool of a political party. Bolt, "A Kuyperian Reflects," 13, asserts that Kuyper "was very clear that the official church was not a political player on the state of human history." Bolt makes the same point in "Abraham Kuyper, Leo XIII," 164. It was Kuyper's position that "Christian political activism...belongs to the church as organism and not to the church as institute" (ibid., footnote 97). Cf., Wood, *Going Dutch*, 173.

11. Murray, "The Relation of Church and State," 255.

12. Ibid., 258.

13. Murray and Kuyper would have agreed with Hashemi's "twin tolerations," articulated in *Islam, Secularism, and Liberal Democracy*, 129. Hashemi summarized what he means by twin tolerations: "Religious institutions should not have a constitutionally guaranteed privilege to dictate, limit, or veto decisions made by democratically elected governments. Likewise, religious groups should have complete autonomy to worship privately *and* advance their private interests in the public square and to sponsor organizations and movements" (124).

beyond the limits of his authority, the duty of the church is "to expose and condemn such a violation of his authority." Furthermore, with respect to laws that are contrary to the moral law of God, the church has the responsibility of opposing them and exposing the evil reflected therein.[14]

The church, however, must do more than denounce sin; it must remind the civil magistrate of his duties, specifically his responsibility to check and oppose tyranny whenever and wherever it raises its ugly head. Murray stood within the mainstream of the Calvinian tradition when he asserted, "When the civil magistrate fails to exercise his God-given authority in the protection and promotion of the obligations, rights, and liberties of the citizens, the church has the right and duty to condemn such inaction, and by its proclamation of the counsel of God to confront the civil magistrate with his responsibility and promote the correction of such neglect."[15] This, of course, is precisely what Calvin did at the conclusion of the *Institutes*. He appealed to the popular magistrates of his time reminding them of their God-given duty to protect the lives and freedom of the people.[16]

A contemporary example of the church instructing the state in the way of righteousness was seen in the work of the Reformed minister D. James Kennedy, pastor at the Coral Ridge Presbyterian Church in Fort Lauderdale, Florida. Reverend Kennedy established the D. James Kennedy Center for Christian Statesmanship in Washington, DC. The Center ministered in a number of ways, but two specifics are particularly noteworthy. First, the Center offered courses through its Statesmanship Institute for our public officials designed to develop Christian thinking with respect to government. The lectures offered by an illustrious faculty included the topics of a Christian worldview, constitutional law, original intent, the Bible and the rule of law, the scriptural foundation of American government, biblical guidelines for government, and social justice and poverty. Secondly, the Center encouraged

14. Murray, "The Relation of Church and State," 255.
15. Ibid.
16. Calvin, *Institutes* IV.20.31.

statesmanship in the bestowal of the annual Distinguished Christian Statesman Award for the purpose of honoring government officials who had exemplified the high standards of righteousness and justice in their public service. Recipients included Representative Marilyn Musgrave, Senator Sam Brownback, and Chief Justice Roy Moore, among others.

As we have argued, the seeds of judicial reform are found in the Bible and its teaching on the state. If the church will commit itself to the faithful preaching of the whole counsel of God, a whole new generation of Christian citizens will arise who understand that they have a strategic role to play in the American republic.

Let us now reflect upon the reform of the courts as it would come from the grassroots

The Christian Citizen

The well-informed Christian citizen operating on the basis of the biblical doctrine of the state—indeed, the Calvinist tradition of political theory—would recognize that tyrannical laws are not valid. He or she would further understand that those who promulgate them cannot be viewed as legitimate rulers.

Calvin referred to laws that are "abhorrent not only to all justice, but also to all humanity and gentleness." How did Calvin regard laws which are contrary to natural law, "that perpetual rule of love?" "I do not think that those barbarous and savage laws," he said, "are to be regarded as laws."[17] Tyrannical laws, in the view of Calvin, had no legitimacy.

This Reformed perspective seems largely to be lost in contemporary public discourse concerning the Supreme Court and law. The idea too often conveyed, to use the language of Kuyper, is that "law is right, not because its contents are in harmony with the eternal principles of right, but because it is *law*. If on the morrow it fixes the very opposite, this also must be right."[18] The Calvin-

---

17. Calvin, *Institutes* IV.20.15.
18. Kuyper, *Lectures on Calvinism*, 89.

ist view, however, is at the heart of the English legal tradition. Sir William Blackstone affirmed that natural law is "superior in obligations to any other" and that "no human laws are of any validity if contrary to this."[19]

Although the mainstream media tend to affirm that the law must be right because it is law—essentially entailing the deification of the state—perceptive Americans think otherwise. Judge Bork recognizes that this is the case and comments that "a very large number of Americans . . . are not deceived by the claim that those results"—coming from the politicization of the law—"are compelled by the actual Constitution." "This perception," Bork observes, "delegitimizes the law in their eyes."[20]

The law is not the only thing that is regarded as illegitimate for large numbers of Americans. The "men in black" are no longer viewed as legitimate by thoughtful Americans. Intelligent citizens cannot regard jurists who twist the Constitution beyond recognition as judges, but rather as tyrants on the bench. Such a perspective is in full continuity with Reformed doctrine. Calvin declared that when the king "exceeded his limits," he in fact "had himself abrogated his power."[21]

This position appears to reflect the medieval idea having its roots in the seventh century in the thought of Isidore of Seville. In his *Etymologiae*, Isidore wrote that "kings are such by ruling." He then elaborated, "For just as a priest is such by sanctification, so a king is king through his ruling." "Therefore the title of king is held by proper administration." "By wrongdoing it is lost."[22] The same

---

19. Blackstone, *Commentaries*, 41.

20. Bork, *The Tempting of America*, 2. Blackstone, *Commentaries*, 42, stated, "Upon these two foundations, the *law of nature* and the *law of revelation* depend all human laws; that is to say, no human law should be suffered to contradict these."

21. Calvin, *Institutes* IV.20.32.

22. Quoted in McIlwain, *The Growth of Political Thought*, 173. A similar distinction between kingship and tyranny is seen in John of Salisbury: "The prince is a kind of likeness of divinity; and the tyrant, on the contrary, a likeness of the boldness of the Adversary, even of the wickedness of Lucifer, imitating him that sought to build his throne to the north and make himself like

idea was taken up again in the thirteenth century in the thought of the English jurist Henry de Bracton who admonished kings to "bestow upon the land what the law bestows upon him, namely rule and power for there is no *rex* where will rules rather than *lex*.[23]

The relevance of Calvinist political theory is obvious: at times federal judges have fallen from their judgeships. As Calvin put it, "Earthly princes lay aside all their power when they rise up against God."[24] Calvin added nothing new when he stated in his sermon on the same biblical passage that such princes "are no longer worth to be counted as princes."[25]

On a practical level, what does this position entail? The implications of Calvinian doctrine are well exemplified in the conduct of Roy Moore the former Chief Justice of Alabama.[26] Judge Moore commissioned and paid for the construction and installation of a monument of the Ten Commandments in the rotunda of the Alabama Judicial Building. No tax dollars were used. Moore was simply acknowledging God and the fundamental truth that legitimate human legislation is ultimately rooted in the moral law of God.

Judge Moore's actions were in the tradition of George Washington who publicly acknowledged God in his First Inaugural Address, stating that his "first official Act" as president would be the "tendering" of "homage to the great Author of every public and private good" and the offering of his "fervent supplications" that the "Almighty Being who rules over the Universe" would give his

---

unto the most High with the exception of his goodness" (*Policraticus* VIII.17). Hallowell, *Main Currents*, 25, makes the observation that "this distinction between true kingship and tyranny runs throughout the political literature of the Middle Ages."

23. Bracton, *On the Laws and Customs*, 33.
24. Calvin, *Commentaries on the Book of the Prophet Daniel*, 382.
25. Cited in Skinner, *The Foundations*, 220.
26. It is quite clear that Judge Moore's refusal to obey the mandate of the Carter appointee Judge Myron Thompson to remove the monument of the Ten Commandments was informed by the medieval and Reformed intellectual heritage. Moore affirms, "When a military commander, a president, or a federal judge sets himself above the law, he has no right to be obeyed; he, in effect, 'unkings' himself. Or, in the case of a federal judge like Myron Thompson, he loses his judicial mantle and becomes a tyrant" (*So Help Me God*, 209).

"benediction" and would "consecrate" the new "Government."[27] His actions were in continuity with the Judiciary Act of 1789 which required all federal judges to acknowledge God when they took their oath of office—the oath ended with the petition "so help me God."[28] Most significantly, his actions were in compliance with the First Amendment[29] which merely declares in its anti-establishment clause that the national government (not the state governments) is prohibited from putting in place a tax-supported national church.[30] Thus, when a United States district court ordered him to remove the monument, Judge Moore refused to obey the federal court order.[31]

Such passive disobedience stands fully within the Calvinian tradition. The first edition of the *Institutes* concluded with this exhortation regarding the "authority of rulers": "We should not enslave ourselves to the wicked desires of men—much less to their impiety."[32] Kuyper spoke similarly, "The Calvinists expressed

---

27. Washington, "First Inaugural Address," 192.

28. Judiciary Act of 1789, currently codified at 28 U.S.C., sec. 453. See Moore, *So Help Me God*, 73.

29. The first clause of the First Amendment reads as follows: "Congress shall make no law respecting an establishment of religion." The legal strategy that Judge Moore's legal team followed in the lawsuit filed against him was quite simple: it would rest on "arguments based on the text of the Constitution." Amazingly, "federal judges are not accustomed" to this kind of argumentation. "We would tell the federal courts," Moore writes, "that I was not *Congress* making a *law* (judges can't make law), that the monument was not an *establishment* of anything, and most importantly that the monument (and my acknowledgment of God) was not *religion*, as defined by the founding fathers and even the Supreme Court" (*So Help Me God*, 180).

30. Berns, *Taking the Constitution Seriously*, 167. It should be remembered that at the time the Constitution was adopted, the states of New Hampshire, Massachusetts, Connecticut, and Maryland had established churches supported by taxes. Cf., McDonald, *Novus Ordo Seclorum*, 43.

31. Judge Moore well understands that what is happening in America is that "federal judges" have "placed themselves above the law": so that "their opinions" are "the new standard of right and wrong" (*So Help Me God*, 1.)

32. Calvin, *Institutes*, 225–26 (1536 edition). "At first glance," Spykman acknowledges, "Romans 13 . . . seems to demand unswerving civil obedience." We have to realize though that "Romans 13 offers a normative picture of the

... the unshakable argument that we should not, *may* not yield to a government which commands a single thing contrary to God and his Word."[33]

The private individual, however, is not allowed to initiate active resistance by taking up arms against the tyrant.[34] By taking this position, Calvin agreed fundamentally with the medieval heritage. The church through the centuries has taken the threat uttered by Jesus with utter seriousness, that all those who take up the sword shall perish by the sword (Matt 26:52).[35] The forbidden action—taking up the sword—meant, as Augustine of Hippo said, "to use weapons against a man's life, without the sanction of the constituted authority."[36] Rather than resorting to an individual act of violence against a tyrant—seen, for example, in the assassination attempt against United States Justice Harry Blackmun, the number one defender of the "constitutional right" to an abortion—the private citizen must pray. We are permitted, Calvin argued, "to implore the Lord's help."[37] To quote from Salisbury, "the method of destroying tyrants which is most useful" is for "those who are oppressed" to lift up "undefiled hands to the Lord to pray devoutly that the scourge wherewith they are afflicted may be turned aside from them."[38]

---

state." In the Romans 13 passage, "we meet civil government as it is meant to be, as it ought to be, as it is called to be." The fact of the matter is that "the state" is "all too often" an "instrument of injustice and corruption." "When the state makes unjust demands, we may be called to resistance" ("The Principled Pluralist," 85).

33. Kuyper, "Calvinism," 308-9.

34. Calvin, *Institutes* IV.20.31.

35. The threat itself, Thomas Aquinas argued in *Summa Theologica* 2a2ae, q.40, art.1, should be understood on two levels—the literal and the metaphorical. For Aquinas, Jesus' statement applied not only to this life, but also to the next: "And yet even those who make sinful use of the sword are not always slain with the sword, yet they always perish with their own sword, because, unless they repent, they are punished eternally for their sinful use of the sword." This quotation is from the five-volume English translation *Summa Theologica*.

36. Augustine, *Reply to Faustus*, XX.70.

37. Calvin, *Institutes* IV.20.29.

38. John of Salisbury, *Policraticus* VIII.20.

We must never forget that social and political renewal in the historical past was accomplished not by acts of violence, but through the prayers and blameless lives of Christian people. To cite one example, we should remember that one of the great changes in history entailed the movement away from the old pagan Roman society to medieval Christendom. Kuyper described the transition in this way: "Christ won and Caesar was toppled. The liberated nations each emerged with its own king, and within those dominions separate spheres, and within those spheres distinct liberties. Then began that glorious life, crowned with nobility, exhibiting in the ever richer organism of guilds and orders and free communities all the energy and glory that sphere sovereignty implies."[39]

It is true, as Kuyper put it, that "the new social order which arose" did not perfectly correspond to "the ideal cherished by Jesus." Nevertheless, he pointed out that we may "acknowledge that *more tolerable* social conditions were born." Kuyper suggested that the moral improvement of medieval Christendom included such elements as greater emphasis in the public mind upon life in the next world rather than the present one, the demolition of the institution of slavery, and the social concern of extending mercy to the poor and the orphans.[40]

---

39. Kuyper, "Sphere Sovereignty," 470.

40. Kuyper, *Christianity*, 30–31. Kuyper made the point, "Common Grace," 198–99, that "terms such as 'a Christian nation,' 'a Christian country,' 'a Christian society,' 'Christian art,' and the like, do not mean that such a nation consists mainly of regenerate Christian persons or that such a society has already been transposed into the kingdom of heaven." Rather, "it means that in such a country special grace in the church and among believers exerted so strong a formative influence on common grace that common grace thereby attained its highest development. The adjective 'Christian' therefore says nothing about the spiritual state of the inhabitants of such a country but only witnesses to the fact that public opinion, the general mind-set, the ruling ideas, the moral norms, the laws and customs there clearly betoken the influence of Christian faith." Practically speaking, "this influence leads to the abolition of slavery in the laws and life of a country, to the improved position of women, to the maintenance of public virtue, respect for the Sabbath, compassion for the poor, consistent regard for the ideal over the material, and—even in manners—the elevation of all that is human from its sunken state to a higher standpoint."

How did such a remarkable thing take place, that pagan Rome gave way to a renewed social order?[41] Such a transformation did not take place over night. It happened through the exemplary lives of ordinary Christians. In Kuyper's thinking, the church as organism encompassing "the whole of regenerate human life" was the agent of social renewal.[42] For the most part, Christians simply went about their daily work. They assembled each Sunday for public worship. They cared for the sick and showed mercy to the poor. "Out of their peacefulness, humility, joy, and mercy, a new world was born."[43]

There are times that we as Christian citizens must refuse obedience to unlawful demands placed upon us by the state. We must speak out against folly and unrighteousness. Our participation in the political process also means that we must vote in appropriate ways in order that there might be resistance to a tyrannical judiciary by the executive and legislative branches of the federal government.

We shall now reflect upon the Calvinist roots of this position and how it would apply to our present situation.

---

41. We must remember, of course, that the renewed social order of medieval Europe was not a golden age of moral perfection. With respect to the issue of church-state relations, the church failed to stay within its boundaries and reached into the sphere of the state and its secular responsibilities. Brownson in *The American Republic* explained why this happened: "In the Middle Ages the State was so barbarously constituted that the church was obliged to supervise its administration, to mix herself up with civil government, in order to infuse some intelligence into civil matters, and to preserve her own rightful freedom and independence" (269).

42. Heslam, *Creating a Christian Worldview*, 133. Wood, *Going Dutch*, 172, asserts, "The organic church took up the church's public responsibilities and received the task of engaging the world directly, where the institution could act only indirectly." Kuyper emphasized the church as organism in his teaching on the church's social responsibility (ibid., 54).

43. Leithart, *The Kingdom and the Power*, 215.

Executive and Legislative Resistance

In the sixteenth century, the Reformed had to contend with the defenders of royal absolutism. Calvin wrote about kings "who seem unrestrained by laws."[44] Beza made reference to those who maintained that "the king is not bound by the laws."[45] He complained that there were people "who so far exalt the authority of kings and supreme rulers as to dare maintain that they have no other Judge but God alone to whom they are bound to render account of their deeds."[46]

Kuyper strongly condemned the divine right of kings theory, expressing "abhorrence for any form of king-worship" and "any cringing before the royal throne."[47] He affirmed that Christ alone has "*absolute* Sovereignty, extending over all things visible and invisible, over the spiritual and the material, all placed in the hands of one *man*." The implications of this biblical position for his political philosophy were significant: "This perfect Sovereignty of the *sinless* Messiah at the same time directly denies and challenges all absolute Sovereignty among *sinful* men on earth, and does so by dividing life into *separate spheres*, each with its own sovereignty."[48]

In the face of absolutist claims on the part of kings, Calvinists have always insisted that kings and emperors are to be restrained by law. Althusius put it this way: "For an emperor to be unable and forbidden to do wicked and prohibited things does not take away from his power or his liberty, but defines the ends and deeds in which his true power and liberty consist." He elaborated, "For it is not the property of imperium that it is able to rule in any manner whatever, nor is it the property of power that it can do anything whatever, but only what agrees with nature and right reason."[49]

---

44. Calvin, *Commentary on the Book of Psalms*, 22.
45. Beza, *Concerning the Rights of Rulers*, 68.
46. Ibid., 64.
47. Kuyper, "Calvinism," 308.
48. Kuyper, "Sphere Sovereignty," 467; italics original.
49. Althusius, *Politica*, 202.

In opposition to the idea that kings possessed a "plenitude of power"[50]—total and complete authority—the Reformed maintained that all political power did not reside in the monarchy. Against the fact of an absolutist monarchy in France, Calvin set forth a counterfact, "an opposing force as real, as worldly, as ordinary as tyranny itself."[51] In France the counterfact could be found in the Estates-General. In England there was the Parliament. Such a distribution of power could be used in defense of liberty.[52]

Calvinists believed that such a counterfact as the Estates-General in France and the Parliament in England were ultimately rooted in the biblical pattern. Beza located the origins of such institutions of the state within the Old Testament itself. The Estates of ancient Israel had a threefold authority. They had the right to choose a king, but they could also depose him, and even punish him. The Estates of Israel "had the authority to choose for themselves from the family of David whom they wished, and afterwards, when he had been elected, either to drive him out or even to execute sentence of death upon him as occasion demanded." As an example of a biblical deposition and execution, Beza cited the uprising of the people of Judah against King Amaziah resulting in his execution, and the installation of Amaziah's son Azariah in his place.[53]

Kuyper likewise affirmed that the constitutional liberties in Calvinist countries were based in the legal system of Israel. He stated, "In the rights of the popular assembly . . . in the particular rights of the tribes and the heads of families, and, most of all, in the manner in which the first king was chosen there lay a basic civic freedom, a breath of fresh air that would wipe out all forms of despotic government."[54]

---

50. Ibid., 192.

51. Walzer, *The Revolution of the Saints*, 59.

52. In the United States, "the separation of the powers of the national government," Bork argues, "have guaranteed our liberties as much as, perhaps more than, the Bill of Rights itself" (*The Tempting of America*, 4).

53. Beza, *Concerning the Rights of Rulers*, 51–52.

54. Kuyper, "Calvinism," 310.

The counterfact of parliamentary bodies in sixteenth-century Europe meant that there was a provision in divine providence for institutional resistance to tyrannical tendencies within the various governments of the time. Commenting upon the Magna Carta, Kuyper spoke about the English Parliament and its acquisition of power such that "it may do everything except make a man a woman." He then added this statement regarding the perspective of God concerning the rights of Parliament that the barons exacted from John Lackland: "That is something He wanted, a right He sanctified."[55]

The Reformed recognized that such a constitutional distribution of power within the European states should be taken advantage of for the purpose of suppressing tyranny. This was the point made by Calvin in his famous discussion of the *populares magistratus* in *Institutes* IV.20.31, calling them "magistrates of the people, appointed to restrain the willfulness of kings." The magistrates of the people were individuals that constituted a representative body which was appointed in an elective manner.[56] Thus Calvin concluded his systematic treatment of theology by instructing the church and the political leaders of his time that popular

---

55. Ibid., 309.

56. Höpfl, *Luther and Calvin*, xli. Calvin left his readers with no ambiguity as to the kind of representative assembly which he had in mind: "As in ancient times the ephors were set against the Spartan kings, or the tribunes of the people against the Roman consuls, or the demarchs against the senate of the Athenians; and perhaps, as things now are, such power as the three estates exercise in every realm when they hold their chief assemblies" (*Institutes* IV.20.31). Here Calvin appealed both to history and to contemporary political theory. Among the ancient Greeks and Romans, he drew attention to individuals who were appointed in an elective manner—the *ephori*, *tribuni plebes*, and *demarche*. Cf., Skinner, *The Foundations*, 232. With respect to his own time, Calvin alluded to the various European parliamentary bodies. His reference to the "three estates" no doubt included the French Estates-General composed of the clergy (the First Estate), the nobles (the Second Estate), and the burghers or townsmen (the Third Estate). The convening of the French Estates-General entailed the election of deputies by each of the respective estates. Cf., Baumgartner, *France in the Sixteenth Century*, 11.

magistrates—in other words, parliamentary bodies—had the duty to "withstand . . . the fierce licentiousness of kings."[57]

Kuyper recognized that Calvin's teaching on the popular magistrates was enormously influential. He declared, "Thus, with Calvin himself lies the origin of the system of secondary powers, of the banner under which Condé rose against Charles, our States against Philip, the English Parliament against the Stuarts, and America's colonies against the mother country." More than that, he insisted that Calvin's doctrine was drawn from the Word of God and that it provided "the glorious principle" from which the constitutional system in the Netherlands was born.[58]

What do the Framers of the Calvinian tradition of political reflection—from Calvin through Kuyper—have to teach us regarding remedies for tyranny as it exists in our American courts? We must remember that the American constitutional system of checks and balances provides a counterfact to the imperial judiciary: the executive and the legislative branches of government.[59]

"A just constitution," Kuyper remarked, "restrains abuse of authority, sets limits, and offers the people a natural protection against lust for power and arbitrariness."[60] We need to remember at this point that the United States Constitution provides for a strong chief executive.[61] This reality is seen in the simple fact that the Constitution places the defense of the Constitution in the hands of the president. In the face of blatant constitutional manipulation

---

57. Calvin, *Institutes* IV.20.31.

58. Kuyper, "Calvinism," 303, 306.

59. It may well be the case that Calvinist teaching on human depravity contributed to the thinking that the separation of powers was a necessity for the new American nation. In his "Farewell Address," 221, Washington referred to "that love of power and proneness to abuse it which predominates in the human heart." The remedy for this defect in human nature is to be found in the "reciprocal checks in the exercise of political power" that is put into place "by dividing and distributing it into different depositories, and constituting each the guardian of the public weal against invasions by the others."

60. Kuyper, "Calvinism," 310.

61. Napolitano, *Constitutional Chaos*, 192. Indeed, the president is "not subject to either of the two branches," the legislative or the judicial.

and attempts to legislate from the bench, the president may simply refuse to enforce flagrantly erroneous rulings from the Court that patently violate the Constitution. He after all has the authority of executive review, the coordinate power to interpret the Constitution, even against conflicting interpretations by the legislative and judicial branches.[62]

Lest we deify the High Court, we must beware of thinking that submission to the Supreme Court must be total and complete.[63] We must also keep in mind that the president is the only officer stipulated in the Constitution who must take an oath to "preserve, protect and defend the Constitution of the United States" (art. 2, sec. 1).[64] The Constitution nowhere states that he must enforce the public policy decisions (legislative activity) of the Supreme Court.

The president may also defend the Constitution in a very practical way by his power of appointing strict constitutionalists to the federal courts.[65] All new judicial appointees must understand

62. See the discussion of the subject of executive review in Kesavan, "Oath of Office," 194-95.

63. Kuyper, "Calvinism," 282, spoke about the danger of the "deification of the state."

64. While the Constitution specifies that the president must take an oath to "preserve, protect and defend the Constitution of the United States," all the persons specified in Article 6—"the Senators and Representatives mentioned, and the Members of the several State Legislatures, and all executive and judicial Officers, both of the United States and of the several States"—must only take a general oath of allegiance "to support this Constitution."

65. Bork forcefully declares, "No person should be nominated or confirmed who does not display a grasp of and devotion to the philosophy of original understanding" (*The Tempting of America*, 9). Indeed, the Constitution itself seems to demand a commitment to a hermeneutic of original understanding in its declaration that "all ... judicial Officers ... of the United States ... shall be bound by Oath or Affirmation, to support this Constitution" (art.6, clause 3). The oath which federal judges take—as the Constitution prescribes—is "to support *this* Constitution." As Bork comments, "*This* Constitution, not one they make up themselves, is to bind federal judges" (174). Meese, "Speech by Attorney General," 76, argues that "a jurisprudence of original intention ... is not difficult to describe." He then explains, "Where the language of the Constitution is specific, it must be obeyed. Where there is a demonstrable consensus among the Framers and ratifiers as to a principle stated or implied by the Constitution, it should be followed. Where there is ambiguity as to the precise

that the Constitution does not give to the judiciary any legislative power and that the function of the federal courts is to apply the law as it comes to them from the Congress.[66]

Such a perspective is in keeping with Reformed teaching on the proper role of a judge. "A good judge," Bullinger contended, "is to determine and pronounce truly and justly, *according to the laws*, what is good, what is evil, what is right, and what is wrong."[67] In this connection, Bucer asked, "For what profit is it to make excellent laws if it is conceded to the judges that they may depart from them according to their good pleasure in making judgments, or even that they interpret laws fraudulently?"[68] Buchanan held that judges "are to administer justice according to the direction of the laws."[69] Rutherford likewise declared that judges "by office must interpret the law, else they cannot give sentence according to . . . equity."[70]

The Constitution also indicates that the congressional power of impeachment provides a check upon malfeasance in the federal courts—specifically, the failure of judges to keep their oath to support the Constitution (art. 6, clause 3) that explicitly declares that "all legislative Powers herein granted shall be vested in a Congress of the United States" (art. 1, sec. 1). The conduct of judges can perhaps be improved by implementing with greater frequency what is essentially the biblical principle of deposition.[71] Tyranny "may be opportunely removed," Althusius declared, by means of the "deposition of the tyrant."[72] With respect to the conduct of judges,

---

meaning or reach of a constitutional provision, it should be interpreted and applied in a manner so as to at least not contradict the text of the Constitution itself."

66. Bork, *The Tempting of America*, 4.
67. Bullinger, *The Decades of Henry Bullinger*, 347; emphasis added.
68. Bucer, *On the Kingdom of Christ*, 376.
69. Buchanan, *The Rights of the Crown in Scotland*, 250.
70. Rutherford, *The Law and the Prince*, 137.
71. Although Congressman Gerald Ford drafted a writ of impeachment against Justice William O. Douglas, associate justice Samuel Chase is the only Supreme Court justice ever to have been impeached. The Senate trial which occurred in 1805 failed to convict him.
72. Althusius, *Politica*, 193.

Bucer affirmed, "Judges should take an oath that they will judge according to the laws, and this must be demanded of them with utmost severity, and those who have manifestly not acted in very good faith should be most severely punished."[73]

Congress should also more often exercise its constitutional right of forbidding the Supreme Court appellate jurisdiction over specific pieces of legislation (art. 3, sec. 2).[74] In addition, constitutional manipulation may be countered by the Congress proposing amendments to the Constitution by a two-thirds vote of the House and Senate followed by the ratification of the legislatures of three fourths of the several states (art. 5).

Calvinist resistance principles would suggest that instances of glaring constitutional reconstruction should be checked with attempts to amend the Constitution.[75] Perhaps the place to start would be an amendment by which voters could recall federal judges who legislate from the bench. As Buchanan put it, "It has been everywhere an invariable usage, that public favours, improperly bestowed, might be reclaimed."[76] California has such a provision by which state court judges may be removed from office by the people.[77] Another amendment which should be implemented would give to Congress the power to override Supreme Court rulings which are nothing more than public policy decisions. This would be similar to the way in which the Congress overrides presidential vetoes—by a two-thirds vote of the House and the Senate (art. 1, sec. 7). Finally, we need to consider an amendment to the Constitution which would require that a ruling of unconstitution-

---

73. Bucer, *On the Kingdom of Christ*, 376.

74. Gold, "Appellate Jurisdiction Clause," 261.

75. Rehnquist, *The Supreme Court*, 319. Washington, in his "Farewell Address," contemplated the possibility that "the spirit of encroachment" would tend to "consolidate the powers of all the departments in one." He further recognized that the amendment procedure provided a means for this problem: "If in the opinion of the people the distribution or modification of the constitutional powers be in any particular wrong, let it be corrected by an amendment in the way which the Constitution designates" (221).

76. Buchanan, *The Rights of the Crown in Scotland*, 273.

77. This is precisely what happened to California Chief Justice Rose Bird.

ality be by a unanimous vote of the Supreme Court—forbidding this power to other federal judges—thereby eliminating dubious narrowly decided cases.

The Recourse of the People

If the president and the Congress fail to resist tyranny in the courts, what recourse do we have as American citizens?

Let us first understand the nature of such a failure. The duty of the magistrates, as Calvin remarked, is "to apply themselves with the highest diligence to prevent the freedom (whose guardians they have been appointed) from being in any respect diminished, far less violated." Calvin then made the pointed charge: "If they are not sufficiently alert and careful, they are faithless in office, and traitors to their country."[78] Let us appreciate the fact that a failure to act, to oppose judicial tyranny, is egregious disloyalty to the Constitution and to the American Republic.

Let us also implore the help of the Lord. Thomas Aquinas, who was influential in the development of Calvinist political thought, said, "Should no human aid whatsoever against a tyrant be forthcoming, recourse must be had to God, the king of all, who is a helper in due time of tribulation."[79] Calvin too believed that prayer is the antidote which may be used in response to the havoc created by tyrants: "It is therefore our bounden duty to beseech him to restore to order what is embroiled in confusion."[80]

There is more though that we can do by virtue of the fact that we live in a republic, which as Calvin noted "is a singular benefit of God."[81] The blessing of a republic means that "the people" have the

---

78. Calvin, *Institutes* IV.20.8.
79. Aquinas, *On Kingship*, I.6.51.
80. Calvin, *Commentary on the Book of Psalms*, 336.
81. Calvin, *Sermons on 1 Samuel*, 67. Kuyper, *Lectures on Calvinism*, 83-84, reflected at length upon Calvin's preference for a republic and the fact that "God has the sovereign power, in the way of his dispersing Providence, to take from a people this most desirable condition, or never to bestow it at all, when a nation is unfit for it, or, by its sin, has utterly forfeited the blessing."

right to "choose, by common consent, their own shepherds."[82] This means that we the people must demand of our presidential candidates that they seek what Bucer called "the reform of the courts."[83] We must insist that they do so by appointing properly qualified judges—in the language of Bucer, persons of "legal ability and virtue" who are "not afraid to offend evil men."[84] Indeed, it "must also be required of judges, that they judge ... according to the meaning germane to the laws."[85] Practically speaking, this means that the failure by the president to appoint originalists to the federal courts or unwillingness by the congress to act as a check on the judiciary must be countered on Election Day with ballots cast for more worthy candidates for high office.

---

82. Calvin, *Commentaries on the Prophet Micah*, 309–10.
83. Bucer, *On the Kingdom of Christ*, 374.
84. Ibid., 375.
85. Ibid., 376.

Conclusion

ABRAHAM KUYPER HAD AN enormous impact on Dutch political life in the nineteenth and twentieth centuries. He organized the Antirevolutionary Party, which had existence from 1879 to 1980.[1] He eventually became prime minister of the Netherlands.[2] The Antirevolutionary Party would play a role in government cabinets for more than a century. "It served as a first line of defense, a kind of retaining wall, against the forces of secularism."[3]

Kuyper was enthusiastic in his description of freedom, as it existed in the United States. The greatest of human liberties, he maintained, was liberty of conscience.[4] The notion of an Inquisition in which people are forced to subscribe to certain beliefs was repugnant to him. "Our Calvinist Theologians and jurists have

---

1. Harinck, "A Historian's Comment," 278. The Antirevolutionary Party was absorbed into the party of the Christian Democrats in 1980.

2. Kuyper was the first Antirevolutionary prime minister in the Netherlands to serve in the twentieth century (1901–1905). Six Antirevolutionary party members would follow him in the office of prime minister. The last was Barend W. Biesheuvel (1971–1973).

3. Van Dyke, "Groen van Prinsterer," 94. Van Dyke specifies, "The Christian parties have insisted on imposing controls and limits to wide-spread demands for state-sponsored gambling, legalization of drugs, abortion on demand, euthanasia by choice, and other symptoms of a rapidly secularizing society. It opened the door to distinctive Christian participation and fostered a pluralist society of mutual tolerance and accommodation" (ibid.).

4. Kuyper, *Lectures on Calvinism*, 108.

defended liberty of conscience against the Inquisition."[5] Liberty of conscience meant that the "conscience is never subject to man but always and ever to God Almighty."[6] "Government," he said, "must" allow "to each and every citizen liberty of conscience, as the primordial and inalienable right of all men."[7]

Liberty of conscience, Kuyper affirmed, is the root from which other liberties spring forth. What is the logical development of what is enshrined in liberty of conscience? The conscience that is bound to God alone has liberty in the realm of ideas, free expression of thought, freedom of speech, and freedom of the press. All of these freedoms are "conclusions which follow from this liberty of conscience."[8] The theological basis for all of these freedoms, Kuyper contended, was to be found in the Reformation of Geneva.[9]

His commitment to the fundamental human right of freedom of religion meant that the distinctively Madisonian approach on church and state resonated within his soul. He wholeheartedly embraced the American approach on disestablishment and religious liberty. This was precisely what he wanted for the Netherlands.

It has been demonstrated in this study that Kuyper was a champion of the enduring principles of political conservatism. He stood in continuity with the central principles of conservatism—in harmony with the trajectory that began with Burke and continued with Reagan. Kuyper believed that his core principles were not only founded upon Calvinism but were actually rooted in the Bible itself. Thus the conservative emphasis upon natural law, the need for limited government, and the importance of freedom has a substantial justification. All three foundational principles in Kuyper's view were based upon the teaching of Holy Scripture. This means that such "principles . . . are eternal, valid for all nations and in force at all times."[10]

5. Ibid., 102.
6. Ibid., 107.
7. Ibid., 108.
8. Ibid.
9. Kuyper, "Calvinism," 286.
10. Kuyper, "Our Program," 255.

Conclusion

Much of our discussion has focused upon the issue of judicial tyranny and a neo-Calvinist approach of resistance and reform initiated by the church and implemented by citizens and the executive and legislative branches of government. This consideration has demonstrated that Kuyper's political thought has power and enduring validity. It needs to be articulated forcefully in the twenty-first century.

Bibliography

Althusius, Johannes. *Politica*. Translated by Frederick S. Carney. Indianapolis: Liberty Fund, 1995.
Aquinas, Thomas. *Aquinas: Selected Political Writings*. Translated by J. W. Dawson. Oxford: Blackwell, 1959.
———. *On Kingship, to the King of Cyprus*. Translated by Gerald B. Phelan. Toronto: Pontifical Institute of Mediaeval Studies, 1982.
Augustine. *Concerning the City of God against the Pagans*. Translated by Henry Bettenson. London: Penguin, 1972.
———. *Reply to Faustus the Manichaean*. Nicene and Post-Nicene Fathers. Edinburgh: T. & T. Clark, 1996.
Balmer, Randall. "Learning from Ivan." *The Reformed Journal* 37/6 (June 1987) 4–5.
Banning, Lance. "James Madison, the Statute for Religious Freedom, and the Crisis of Republican Convictions." In *The Virginia Statute for Religious Freedom*, edited by Merrill D. Peterson and Robert C. Vaughan, 108–38. Cambridge: Cambridge University Press, 1988.
Baumgartner, Frederick J. *France in the Sixteenth Century*. New York: St. Martin's, 1995.
Belz, Herman. "Abraham Lincoln." In *American Conservatism: An Encyclopedia*, edited by Bruce Frohnen et al., 514–18. Wilmington, DE: ISI, 2006.
Berkhof, Louis. *The Church and Social Problems*. Grand Rapids: Eerdmans-Sevensma, 1913.
Berman, Paul. *Terror and Liberalism*. New York: Norton, 2004.
Berns. Walter. *Taking the Constitution Seriously*. New York: Simon and Schuster, 1987.
Beversluis, Eric H. "Backwards Theology." *The Reformed Journal* 35/2 (February 1985) 3–4.
Beza, Theodore. *Concerning the Rights of Rulers over Their Subjects and the Duty of Subjects toward Their Rulers*. Translated by Henri-Louis Gonin. Pretoria: H.A.U.M., 1956.

Bibliography

Blackstone, William. *Commentaries on the Laws of England 1.* Facs. ed. Chicago: University of Chicago Press, 1979.
Boer, Harry R. "So Hollow a Figure." *The Reformed Journal* 39/2 (February 1989) 2-3.
Bolt, John. "Abraham Kuyper and the Holland-America Line of Liberty." *Journal of Markets and Morality* 1/1 (Spring 1998) 35-59.
———. "Abraham Kuyper and the Search for an Evangelical Public Theology." In *Evangelicals in the Public Square*, edited by J. Budziszewski, 141-61. Grand Rapids: Baker, 2006.
———. "Abraham Kuyper, Leo XIII, Walter Rauschenbusch, and the Search for an American Public Theology." In *Religion, Pluralism, and Public Life: Abraham Kuyper's Legacy for the Twenty-First Century*, edited by Luis E. Lugo, 145-72. Grand Rapids: Eerdmans, 2000.
———. *A Free Church, A Holy Nation.* Grand Rapids: Eerdmans, 2001.
———. "A Kuyperian Reflects on Father Abraham and the 'Religious Right.'" *Perspectives* 23/6 (June-July 2008) 9-13.
Bork, Robert H. *Slouching Towards Gomorrah: Modern Liberalism and American Decline.* New York: Harper Collins, 1996.
———. *The Tempting of America: The Political Seduction of the Law.* New York: Free Press, 1990.
Bozeman, Theodore Dwight. "Inductive and Deductive Politics: Science and Society in Antebellum Presbyterian Thought." *The Journal of American History* 64/3 (1977) 704-22.
———. *Protestants in an Age of Science: The Baconian Ideal and Antebellum American Religious Thought.* Chapel Hill, NC: The University of North Carolina Press, 1977.
Bracton, Henry de. *On the Laws and Customs of England.* 2 vols. Cambridge, MA: Belknap, 1968.
Bratt, James D. *Abraham Kuyper: Modern Calvinist, Christian Democrat.* Grand Rapids: Eerdmans, 2013.
Brinks, Herbert J. "The Unlikely Heretic." *The Reformed Journal* 37/1 (January 1987) 4.
Brownson, Orestes. A. *The American Republic.* Wilmington, DE: ISI, 2003.
Bucer, Martin. *On the Kingdom of Christ.* Edited by Wilhelm Pauck. Library of Christian Classics. Philadelphia: Westminster, 1969.
Buchanan, George. *The Rights of the Crown in Scotland.* Harrisonburg, VA: Sprinkle, 1982.
Buckley, William F. *Up from Liberalism.* Rev. ed. New York: Stein and Day, 1984.
Bullinger, Henry. *The Decades of Henry Bullinger.* Translated by H. I. Cambridge: Cambridge University Press, 1849.
Burke, Edmund. *The Philosophy of Edmund Burke.* Edited by Louis Bredvold and Ralph Ross. Ann Arbor: University of Michigan Press, 1960.
———. *Reflections on the Revolution in France.* New York: Holt, Rinehart, and Winston, 1962.

BIBLIOGRAPHY

———. *The Works and Correspondence of Edmund Burke.* Vol. 3. London: Gilbour and Rivington, 1852.
Calvin, John. *Calvin's Commentaries.* Edinburgh: Calvin Translation Society, 1843–55. Reprint. Grand Rapids: Baker, 1979.
———. *Institutes of the Christian Religion.* 1536 ed. Translated by Ford Lewis Battles. Grand Rapids: Eerdmans, 1986.
———. *Institutes of the Christian Religion.* 1559 ed. Translated by Ford Lewis Battles. Philadelphia: Westminster, 1960.
Chadwick, Owen. *The Reformation.* New York: Penguin, 1972.
Chayes, Abraham. "The Role of the Judge in Public Law Litigation." *Harvard LawReview* 89/7 (May 1976) 1281–316.
Clarke, Erskine. *Our Southern Zion: A History of Calvinism in the South Carolina Low Country: 1690–1990.* Tuscaloosa: The University of Alabama Press, 1996.
Conser, Walter H. *Church and Confession: Conservative Theologians in Germany, England, and America, 1815–1866.* Macon, GA: Mercer University Press, 1984.
Cottret, Bernard. *Calvin: A Biography.* Translated by M. Wallace McDonald. Grand Rapids: Eerdmans, 2000.
Dabney, Robert L. "The Christian Soldier." In *Discussions: Evangelical and Theological,* 1:614–25. Edinburgh: Banner of Truth, 1982.
———. "Civic Ethics." In *Discussions: Evangelical and Theological,* 3:100–126. Edinburgh: Banner of Truth, 1982.
———. *Systematic Theology.* Edinburgh: Banner of Truth, 1985.
Davis, James Calvin. *On Religious Liberty: Selections from the Works of Roger Williams.* Cambridge, MA: Belknap, 2008.
Dennison, William D. "Dutch Neo-Calvinism and the Roots for Transformation: An Introductory Essay." *Journal of the Evangelical Theological Society* 42/2 (June 1999) 271–91.
Drakeman, Donald L. "Religion and the Republic: James Madison and the First Amendment." *Journal of Church and State* 25/3 (Autumn 1983) 427–45.
Dunn, Charles W., and J. David Woodard. *The Conservative Tradition in America.* Lanham, MD: Rowman and Littlefield, 1996.
Durham, W. Cole, and Elizabeth A. Sewell. "Virginia Founders and the Birth of Freedom." In *Lectures on Religion and the Founding of the Republic,* edited by John W. Welch, 67–76. Provo, UT: Brigham Young University, 2003.
Eastland, Terry. "A Court Tilting Against Religious Liberty." In *"A Country I Do Not Recognize": The Legal Assault on American Values,* edited by Robert H. Bork, 85–111. Stanford: Hoover Institution, 2005.
Emmerich, Charles J. "The Enigma of James Madison on Church and State." In *Religion, Public Life, and the American Polity,* edited by Luis E. Lugo, 51–73. Knoxville: University of Tennessee Press, 1994.
Feldman, Noah. *The Fall and Rise of the Islamic State.* Princeton:Princeton University Press, 2008.

Frohnen, Bruce, ed. *The American Republic: Primary Sources*. Indianapolis: Liberty Fund, 2002.

Gold, Andrew S. "Appellate Jurisdiction Clause." In *The Heritage Guide to the Constitution*, edited by Edwin Meese, 258–61. Washington, DC: Regnery, 2005.

Goldwater, Barry. *The Conscience of a Conservative*. Washington, DC: Regnery Gateway, 1990.

Graglia, Lino A. "Constitutional Law without the Constitution: The Supreme Court's Remaking of America." In *"A Country I Do Not Recognize": The Legal Assault on American Values*, edited by Robert H. Bork, 1–55. Stanford: Hoover Institution, 2005.

Graham, Gordon. "Kuyper, Neo-Calvinism, and Contemporary Political Philosophy." *The Kuyper Center Review: New Essays in Reformed Theology and Public Life* 1 (2010) 50–60.

Graham, W. Fred. *The Constructive Revolutionary: John Calvin and His Socio-Economic Impact*. Richmond: John Knox, 1971.

Groen van Prinsterer, William. *Lectures on Unbelief and Revolution*. St. Catherines, ON: Paideia, 1989.

Hall, David W. "A Response to Johan D. van der Vyver's 'The Jurisprudential Legacy of Abraham Kuyper and Leo XIII.'" *Journal of Markets and Morality* 5/1 (Spring 2002) 251–75.

Hallowell, John H. *Main Currents in Modern Political Thought*. New York: Holt, Rinehart, and Winston, 1950.

Handy, Robert T. "The Magna Charta of Religious Freedom in America." *Union Seminary Quarterly Review* 38/3–4 (1984) 301–17.

Harbour, William. *The Foundations of Conservative Thought: An Anglo-American Tradition in Perspective*. Notre Dame: University of Notre Dame Press, 1982.

Harinck, George. "Abraham Kuyper's Historical Understanding and Reformed Historiography." *Fides et Historia* 37/1 (Winter–Spring 2005) 71–82.

———. "A Historian's Comment on the Use of Abraham Kuyper's Idea of Sphere Sovereignty." *Journal of Markets and Morality* 5/1 (Spring 2002) 277–84.

Hashemi, Nader. *Islam, Secularism, and Liberal Democracy: Toward a Democratic Theory for Muslim Societies*. Oxford: Oxford University Press, 2009.

Heslam, Peter S. *Creating a Christian Worldview: Abraham Kuyper's Lectures on Calvinism*. Grand Rapids: Eerdmans, 1998.

———. "Prophet of a Third Way: The Shape of Kuyper's Socio-Political Vision." *Journal of Markets and Morality* 5/1 (Spring 2002) 11–33.

Hexham, Irving. "Christian Politics according to Abraham Kuyper." *Crux* 19/1 (March 1983) 2–7.

Hill, Samuel S. *The South and North in American Religion*. Athens, GA: University of Georgia Press, 1980.

Bibliography

Höpfl, Harro, ed. and trans. *Luther and Calvin on Secular Authority*. Cambridge: Cambridge University Press, 1991.

Howard, A. E. Dick. "James Madison and the Founding of the Republic." In *James Madison on Religious Liberty*, edited by Robert S. Alley, 21–34. Buffalo: Prometheus, 1985.

Hunt, Gaillard. *Life of James Madison*. New York: Doubleday, 1902.

Jellema, Dirk W. "Abraham Kuyper's Answer to 'Liberalism.'" *Reformed Journal* 15/5 (May–June 1965) 10–14.

John of Salisbury. *Policraticus*. Abridged ed. New York: Frederick Unger, 1979.

Kasteel, Piet. *Abraham Kuyper*. Kampen: Kok, 1938.

Kendall, Willmoore, and George Carey. "Towards a Definition of Conservatism." *The Journal of Politics* 26/2 (May 1964) 406–22.

Kengor, Paul. *God and Ronald Reagan*. New York: HarperCollins, 2004.

Kesavan, Vasan. "Oath of Office." In *The Heritage Guide to the Constitution*, edited by Edwin Meese, 194–95. Washington, DC: Regnery, 2005.

Ketcham, Ralph. *James Madison: A Biography*. Newtown, CT: American Political Biography, 1971.

———. "James Madison and Religion—A New Hypothesis." *Journal of the Presbyterian Historical Society* 38/2 (June 1960) 65–90.

Kilpatrick, James J. *The Sovereign States: Notes of a Citizen of Virginia*. Chicago: Regnery, 1957.

Kingdon, Robert M. "The Political Resistance of the Calvinists in France and the Low Countries." *Church History* 27 (1958) 220–33.

Kirk, Russell. *The Conservative Mind*. Chicago: Regnery, 1953.

———. *Edmund Burke: A Genius Reconsidered*. Wilmington, DE: ISI, 1997.

———. *The Politics of Prudence*. Bryn Mawr, PA: ISI, 1993.

———. *The Portable Conservative Reader*. New York: Penguin, 1982.

Kuyper, Abraham. "Calvinism: Source and Stronghold of Our Constitutional Liberties." In *Abraham Kuyper: A Centennial Reader*, edited by James D. Bratt, 279–317. Grand Rapids: Eerdmans, 1998.

———. *Christianity and the Class Struggle*. Translated by Dirk Jellema. Grand Rapids: Piet Hein, 1950.

———. "Common Grace." In *Abraham Kuyper: A Centennial Reader*, edited by James D. Bratt, 165–201. Grand Rapids: Eerdmans, 1998.

———. *Common Grace: Noah-Adam*. Translated by Nelson D. Kloosterman and Ed M. van der Maas. Grand Rapids: Christian's Library, 2013.

———. "Conservatism and Orthodoxy: False and True Preservation." In *Abraham Kuyper: A Centennial Reader*, edited by James D. Bratt, 65–85. Grand Rapids: Eerdmans, 1998.

———. "Freedom." In *Abraham Kuyper: A Centennial Reader*, edited by James D. Bratt, 317–22. Grand Rapids: Eerdmans, 1998.

———. *Kuyper in America*. Translated by Dagmire Houniet. Sioux Center, IA: Dordt College Press, 2012.

———. *Lectures on Calvinism*. Grand Rapids: Eerdmans, 1931.

BIBLIOGRAPHY

———. "Maranatha." In *Abraham Kuyper: A Centennial Reader*, edited by James D. Bratt, 205–29. Grand Rapids: Eerdmans, 1998.

———. "Our Program." In *Political Order and Plural Structure of Society*, edited by James W. Skillen and Rockne M. McCarthy, 242–57. Translated by Harry der Nederlander. Atlanta: Scholars, 1991.

———. *Rooted and Grounded: The Church as Organism and Institution*. Translated by Nelson D. Kloosterman. Grand Rapids: Christian's Library, 2013.

———. "Sphere Sovereignty." In *Abraham Kuyper: A Centennial Reader*, edited by James D. Bratt, 461–90. Grand Rapids: Eerdmans, 1998.

Labunski, Richard. *James Madison and the Struggle for the Bill of Rights*. Oxford: Oxford University Press, 2006.

Langley, McKendre R. "Emancipation and Apologetics: The Foundation of Abraham Kuyper's Anti-Revolutionary Party in the Netherlands, 1872–1880." PhD diss., Westminster Theological Seminary, 1995.

Lawlor, George L. *The Beatitudes Are for Today*. Grand Rapids: Baker, 1974.

Leithart, Peter J. *The Kingdom and the Power*. Phillipsburg, NJ: Presbyterian and Reformed, 1993.

Levin, Mark R. *Men in Black: How the Supreme Court Is Destroying America*. Washington, DC: Regnery, 2005.

Lewis, Bernard. *The Crisis of Islam: Holy War and Unholy Terror*. New York: Random House, 2003.

Locke, John. *A Letter Concerning Toleration*. Indianapolis: Hackett, 1983.

Loconte, Joseph. "Faith and the Founding: The Influence of Religion in the Politics of James Madison." *Journal of Church and State* 45/4 (Autumn 2003) 699–715.

Little, David. "Religious Liberty." In *Christianity and Law: An Introduction*, edited by John Witte and Frank S. Alexander, 249–70. Cambridge: Cambridge University Press, 2008.

Lucas, Sean Michael. "Southern-Fried Kuyper? Robert Lewis Dabney, Abraham Kuyper, and the Limitations of Public Theology." *Westminster Theological Journal* 61/1 (Spring 2004) 179–201.

Machen, J. Gresham. *Education, Christianity, and the State*. Edited by John W. Robbins. Jefferson, MD: Trinity Foundation, 1987.

Madison, James. "Memorial and Remonstrance." In *Church and State in American History*, edited by John F. Wilson and Donald L. Drakeman, 63–68. Boulder, CO: Westview, 2008.

Martyr, Justin. *Dialogue with Trypho*. The Ante-Nicene Fathers. Edinburgh: T. & T. Clark, 1989.

McDonald, Forrest. *Novus Ordo Seclorum: The Intellectual Origins of the Constitution*. Lawrence: University Press of Kansas, 1985.

McDowell, Gary L. "The Perverse Paradox of Privacy." In *"A Country I Do Not Recognize": The Legal Assault on American Values*, edited by Robert H. Bork, 57–83. Stanford: Hoover Institution, 2005.

BIBLIOGRAPHY

McGoldrick, James E. *God's Renaissance Man: The Life and Work of Abraham Kuyper*. Darlington: Evangelical, 2000.

McGrath, Alister. *A Life of John Calvin: A Study in the Shaping of Western Culture*. Oxford: Blackwell, 1990.

McIlwain, Charles H. *The Growth of Political Thought in the West: From the Greeks to End of the Middle Ages*. New York: Macmillan, 1932.

Meese, Edwin. "Speech by Attorney General Edwin Meese, III, before the Federalist Society Lawyers Division." In *Originalism: A Quarter-Century of Debate*, edited by Steven G. Calabresi, 71–82. Washington, DC: Regnery, 2007.

Miller, Perry. *The New England Mind: From Colony to Province*. Cambridge, MA: Harvard University Press, 1953.

Moore, Roy. *So Help Me God: The Ten Commandments, Judicial Tyranny, and the Battle for Religious Freedom*. Nashville: Broadman and Holman, 2005.

Mouw, Richard J. *Abraham Kuyper: A Short and Personal Introduction*. Grand Rapids: Eerdmans, 2011.

———. "Some Reflections on Sphere Sovereignty." In *Religion, Pluralism, and Public Life: Abraham Kuyper's Legacy for the Twenty-First Century*, edited by Luis E. Lugo, 87–109. Grand Rapids: Eerdmans, 2000.

Murray, John. "The Relation of Church and State." In *Collected Writings of John Murray*, 1:253–59. Edinburgh: Banner of Truth, 1976.

Nagel, Paul C. "Madison the Intellectual." In *James Madison on Religious Liberty*, edited by Robert S. Alley, 313–14. Buffalo: Prometheus, 1985.

Napolitano, Andrew P. *Constitutional Chaos*. Nashville: Nelson, 2004.

Nash, Ronald H. *Life's Ultimate Questions: An Introduction to Philosophy*. Grand Rapids: Zondervan, 1999.

Niebuhr, Richard. *Christ and Culture*. New York: Harper and Row, 1951.

Nisbet, Robert. *Conservatism: Dream and Reality*. Minneapolis: University of Minnesota Press, 1986.

Noll, Mark. "What Has Been Distinctly American about American Presbyterians?" *Journal of Presbyterian History* 84/1 (Spring–Summer 2006) 6–11.

Noonan, Peggy. *When Character Was King: A Story of Ronald Reagan*. New York: Penguin, 2001.

Novak, Michael. "The Wisdom of Madison." In *James Madison on Religious Liberty*, edited by Robert S. Alley, 299–302. Buffalo: Prometheus, 1985.

Oakeshott, Michael J. *Rationalism in Politics and Other Essays*. Rev. ed. Indianapolis: Liberty, 1991.

O'Donovan, Oliver, and Joan Lockwood O'Donovan. *From Irenaeus to Grotius: A Sourcebook in Christian Political Thought, 100–1625*. Grand Rapids: Eerdmans, 1999.

Parker, T. H. L. *John Calvin*. Sydney: Lion, 1975.

Pfeffer, Leo. "Madison's 'Detached Memoranda': Then and Now." In *The Virginia Statute for Religious Freedom*, edited by Merrill D. Peterson and Robert C. Vaughan, 283–312. Cambridge: Cambridge University Press, 1988.

Reagan, Ronald. *Abortion and the Conscience of a Nation.* Nashville: Thomas Nelson, 1984.
———. *Reagan: A Life in Letters.* Edited by Kiron K. Skinner et al. New York: Free Press, 2003.
Rehnquist, William H. *The Supreme Court: How It Was, How It Is.* New York: William Morrow, 1987.
Rhode, Deborah L. "A Tale to Justice Thurgood Marshall: Letting the Law Catch Up." *Stanford Law Review* 44 (1992) 1259–66.
Riemer, Neal. "Madison: A Founder's Vision of Religious Liberty and Public Life." In *Religion, Public Life and the American Polity,* edited by Louis E. Lugo, 37–50. Knoxville: University of Tennessee Press, 1994.
Rossiter, Clinton. *Conservatism in America.* 2nd ed. Cambridge, MA: Harvard University Press, 1982.
Rutherford, Samuel. *The Law and the Prince.* Harrisonburg, VA: Sprinkle, 1982.
Schaff, Philip. "Church and State in the United States." In *Church and State in American History,* edited by John F. Wilson and Donald L. Drakeman, 147–50. Boulder, CO: Westview, 2003.
Schreiner, Susan E. *The Theater of His Glory: Nature and the Natural Order in the Thought of John Calvin.* Durham, NC: Labyrinth, 1991.
Schweikert, Larry, and Michael Allen. *A Patriot's History of the United States.* New York: Sentinel, 2004.
Sherratt, Timothy. "Rehabilitating the State in America: Abraham Kuyper's Overlooked Contribution." In *Re-enchantment of Political Science,* edited by Thomas W. Heilke and Ashley Woodiwiss, 121–48. Lanham, MD: Lexington, 2001.
Sigler, Jay A. *The Conservative Tradition in American Thought.* New York: Putnam's, 1969.
Skillen, James W. "Politics, Pluralism, and the Ordinances of God." In *Life Is Religion,* edited by Henry Vander Goot, 195–206. St. Catherines, ON: Paidea, 1981.
Skinner, Quentin. *The Foundations of Modern Political Thought.* 2 vols. Cambridge: Cambridge University Press, 1978.
Smith, Gary S. *The Universe, Society, and Ethics.* Vol. 2, *Building a Christian Worldview.* Edited by W. Andrew Hoffecker. Phillipsburg, NJ: Presbyterian and Reformed, 1988.
Spitz, Lewis W. *The Protestant Reformation: 1517–1559.* New York: Harper, 1985.
Spykman, Gordon J. "The Principled Pluralist Position." In *God and Politics,* edited by Gary S. Smith, 78–99. Phillipsburg, NJ: Presbyterian and Reformed, 1989.
Thornwell, James H. "Address to All Churches of Christ." In *The Collected Writings of James Henley Thornwell,* 4:446–64. Edinburgh: Banner of Truth, 1974.
———. "Sermon on National Sins." In *The Collected Writings of James Henley Thornwell,* 4:510–48. Edinburgh: Banner of Truth, 1974.

BIBLIOGRAPHY

Troeltsch, Ernst. *The Social Teaching of the Christian Church*. Translated by Olive Wyon. London: Allen and Unwin, 1931.
Vander Hart, Mark. "Abraham Kuyper and the Theonomy Debate." *Mid-America Journal of Theology* 2/1 (1986) 63-77.
van der Kroef, Justus M. "Abraham Kuyper and the Rise of Neo-Calvinism in the Netherlands." *Church History* 17/4 (December 1948) 316-44.
VanDrunen, David. "Abraham Kuyper and the Reformed Natural Law and Two Kingdoms Traditions." *Calvin Theological Journal* 42 (2007) 283-307.
Van Dyke, Harry. "Groen van Prinsterer: Godfather of Bavinck and Kuyper." *Calvin Theological Journal* 47 (2012) 72-97.
Van Geest, Fred. "Democracy and the Neo-Calvinist Tradition." *Christian Scholars Review* 37/1 (Fall 2007) 47-76.
Van Til, Kent A. "Abraham Kuyper and Michael Walzer: The Justice of the Spheres." *Calvin Theological Journal* 40 (2005) 267-89.
Wallace, Ronald S. *Calvin, Geneva and the Reformation: A Study of Calvin as Social Reformer, Churchman, Pastor and Theologian*. Edinburgh: Scottish Academic, 1988.
Walton, Robert C. *Zwingli's Theocracy*. Toronto: University of Toronto Press, 1967.
Walzer, Michael. *The Revolution of the Saints: A Study in the Origin of Radical Politics*. Cambridge, MA: Harvard University Press, 1965.
Washington, George. "Farewell Address." In *An American Primer*, edited by Daniel J. Boorstin, 211-29. New York: Mentor, 1966.
———. "First Inaugural Address." In *An American Primer*, edited by Daniel J. Boorstin, 189-95. New York: Mentor, 1966.
Wells, Ronald A. "Kinder and Gentler." *The Reformed Journal* 39/1 (January 1989) 2-3.
———. "Taking Stock of Reagan." *The Reformed Journal* 37/11 (November 1987) 2-3.
West, Thomas G. "Religious Liberty: The View from the Founding." In *On Faith and Free Government*, edited by Daniel C. Palm, 3-27. Lanham, MD: Rowman and Littlefield, 1997.
Whitehead, John. *The Second American Revolution*. Wheaton, IL: Crossway, 1982.
Wills, Garry. *James Madison*. New York: Henry Holt, 2002.
Wintle, Michael. *Pillars of Piety: Religion in the Netherlands in the Nineteenth Century, 1813-1901*. Hull: Hull University Press, 1987.
Witte, John. "The Biography and Biology of Liberty: Abraham Kuyper and the American Experiment." In *Religion, Pluralism, and Public Life: Abraham Kuyper's Legacy for the Twenty-First Century*, edited by Luis E. Lugo, 243-62. Grand Rapids: Eerdmans, 2000.
———. "God's Joust, God's Justice: The Revelations of Legal History." *The Princeton Seminary Bulletin* 20/3 (1999) 295-313.
———. *Religion and the American Constitutional Experiment*. 2nd ed. Boulder, CO: Westview, 2005.

Bibliography

Wolterstorff, Nicholas P. "Abraham Kuyper (1837–1920)." In *The Teachings of Modern Protestantism on Law, Politics, and Human Nature*, edited by John Witte, 29–69. New York: Columbia University Press, 2007.

———. "An Open Letter to Ed Ericson." *The Reformed Journal* 35/10 (October 1985) 2–4.

Wood, John Halsey. *Going Dutch in the Modern Age: Abraham Kuyper's Struggle for a Free Church in the Nineteenth-Century Netherlands*. Oxford: Oxford University Press, 2013.

Subject Index

Abington v. Schempp, 68
Althusius, Johannes, 28, 86, 91
Ambrose, Bishop, 52n18
American Conservatism, 3n9
Anglican priests, 56–57
Antirevolutionary Party, 6, 8, 39, 95
Aquinas, Thomas, 54, 83n35, 93
Augustine, 83

Baptist preachers, 56
Beza, Theodore, 86
Black, Hugo, 67n42, 68n44
Blackmun, Harry, 83
Blasphemy, 52n16
Bolt, John, 2n7, 77n10
Bork, Robert, 66n37, 87n52, 90n65
Bracton, Henry de, 81
British Conservatism, 3n9
Brownson, Orestes, 27n18, 34n1, 50n10, 85n41
Bucer, Martin, 72, 91–92, 94
Buchanan, George, 91–92
Buckley, William F., 1, 19, 27
Bullinger, Henry, 71, 91
Burke, Edmund, 2–4, 7, 13–14

caesaro-papism, 36n8
Calvin, John, 41–45, 70–72, 76, 79–80, 88–89, 93–94
Chrysostom, Archbishop, 52n18

church disestablishment, 37, 46, 55–58
church establishment, 44
church-state separation, 37n15
Cicero, 9n51
common grace, 18–19, 84n40
Communism, 19
conservateur, 4
contract theories, 21n52
constitutionalism, 25–26

Dabney, Robert, 21n52, 44n49
Declaration of Independence, 16, 67
delegated powers, 26
Democratic Party, 6
despotism, 54–55
Dutch Conservative Party, 6
Dutch Republic, 40–41

Engale v. Vitale, 68
equal rights, 50–51
Erastianism, 51
Estates-General, 87, 88n56
eternal law, 16
Eusebius of Caesarea, 52n18
Everson v. Board of Education, 67n42
executive review, 90

false conservatism, 9

109

Subject Index

Federalism, 5n21, 28n26
First Amendment, 36, 45–47, 82
First Table of the Law, 52n17
free church, 58n44
French Revolution, 4, 8, 13n4, 28n29, 38–39

Gelasius, Pope, 43n42
Goldwater, Barry, 1, 20–21, 23, 26

Henry, Patrick, 56
holy commonwealth, 41n36
Holy Scripture, 10–12, 96

illegitimate law, 79–80
institutional church, 74n2, 75n4
Isidore of Seville, 80

Jefferson, Thomas, 6
John of Salisbury, 80n22, 83
judicial tyranny, 64–69
justice, 24–25
Justin Martyr, 61
Justinian, Emperor, 44n45, 51

Kennedy, Anthony, 66 67
Kennedy, D. James, 78–79
Kilpatrick, James, 27–28
Kirk, Russell, 1, 3n9, 14–15

Lawrence v. Texas, 66
legal positivism, 16
liberalism, 68–69
liberty of conscience, 35–36, 49–50, 62, 96
Lincoln, Abraham, 7
localism, 27–29
Locke, John, 11n59, 47n58

Machen, Gresham, 72–73
Madison, James, 45–58
Marshall, John, 65n34
Mason, George, 48
Massachusetts Bay, 42

Mather, Cotton, 49n4
Mather, Increase, 42
Meese, Edwin, 90n65
Moore, Roy, 65, 68, 81–82
moral depravity, 17–18
Muhammad, 43n43
Murray, John, 77–78

Napoleon, 4
natural law, 12–13, 16–17
neo-Calvinism, 9

Oakeshott, Michael, 4–5, 24
organic church, 74n2

Paine, Thomas, 48n1
Parliament, 87–88
passive disobedience, 82–83
persecution, 57
populares magistratus, 88–89
pure democracy, 14n9

radicalism, 19–20
Reagan, Ronald, 1–3, 69n49, 72n67
Rehnquist, William, 65, 68
religious pluralism, 39n26
religious toleration, 48n1
Republican Party, 7
Reveil party, 74n1
Roe v. Wade, 69–70

Schaff, Philip, 46
Servetus, Michael, 8n42, 44–45
Shari'a, 10n53
Shia Iran, 10n53
socialism, 24
social morality, 13–16
social transformation, 39n28, 60–62
Spanish Inquisition, 53n21
sphere sovereignty, 30–32
Statute for Religious Freedom, 56
Stone v. Graham, 68

Taliban, 10n53

Subject Index

theocracy, 10n53, 43n44
theonomy, 10–11
Thornwell, James, 15n14, 22n55, 75n4
totalitarianism, 23, 62n14
true conservatism, 6n22
twin tolerations, 11n59, 77n13
two-sphere doctrine, 43–44
tyranny, 62–64

unalienable rights, 49–50, 53

Virginia Bill of Rights, 48

war, 25
Washington, George, 66n35, 81–82, 89n59, 92n75
William I, King, 41n33
Williams, Roger, 47n58

www.ingramcontent.com/pod-product-compliance
Lightning Source LLC
Chambersburg PA
CBHW070927160426
43193CB00011B/1597